DISAPPEAR FOR SIX MONTHS

Become a Ghost, Do These Things and Return Unrecognizable

Samuel Emmanuel

This book is a work of non-fiction. The views expressed within are solely those of the author and do not necessarily reflect the views of any organizations or individuals mentioned or referenced in this book.

actions or results that arise from the use or implementation of the information provided in this book.

While every effort has been made to ensure that the information in this book is up to date and relevant, readers should be aware that the self-development field is constantly evolving. New information and research may emerge that could modify or alter the understanding or applicability of the concepts presented in this book. The author and publisher do not assume any responsibility for updating the content to reflect such developments.

Table of Contents

.

Introduction

In the vast tapestry of human existence, there lies an uncharted territory brimming with untapped potential and boundless possibilities - the realm of self-development. Welcome to a transformative journey where the power to redefine your life rests firmly in your hands.

Within these pages, we invite you to embark on a profound exploration of your innermost self - an expedition that will lead you to discover the depths of your true potential and the boundless reservoir of strength that lies within. This is not just another self-help book; it is a guide to unlocking the doorways to growth, empowerment, and purpose.

Life's journey can often feel like navigating through a labyrinth of challenges, dreams, and uncertainties. At times, we find ourselves imprisoned by limiting beliefs, insecurities, and fears, unable to break free from the invisible chains that hold us back. But deep within each of us lies an unshakable force, a beacon of light yearning to illuminate the path to greatness.

The quest for self-development is not about seeking perfection, nor is it about emulating someone else's journey. Instead, it is an expedition that calls for authenticity, vulnerability, and the audacity to embrace our imperfections. It is about peeling back the layers of conditioning that society and life's experiences have placed upon us, and revealing the raw essence of who we truly are.

Throughout this book, you will encounter an arsenal of empowering tools, time-tested wisdom, and transformative insights. Drawing from ancient philosophies and cutting-edge research, you will embark on a voyage through the unexplored territories of the mind, body, and spirit. Prepare to challenge your beliefs, expand your horizons, and rewrite the narratives that have shaped your life.

As you traverse this path of self-discovery, you will encounter hurdles and obstacles, but fear not, for these challenges are the very crucibles that forge resilience and wisdom. With every obstacle surmounted, you will emerge wiser, stronger, and more equipped to face life's uncertainties with a newfound sense of purpose.

But remember, self-development is not a destination; it is an ever-evolving journey. Each day is an opportunity to learn, grow, and reinvent ourselves. With every page you read and every exercise you undertake, you will inch closer to becoming the architect of your destiny, the conductor of your life's symphony.

So, dear seeker of greatness, if you are ready to unlock the doors that lead to your true potential, if you are prepared to confront your fears and embrace your authentic self, then turn the pages and embark on this empowering odyssey. Together, we shall uncover the infinite possibilities that lie within you, and pave the way to a life of purpose, fulfillment, and boundless self-discovery. The journey begins now.

Chapter 1: Work Towards Financial Independence

Financial independence, a state where an individual no longer relies on a paycheck to cover their basic needs and expenses, is a dream shared by many. It represents a path to freedom, choice, and security, allowing individuals to pursue their passions, retire early, or weather unforeseen financial storms with confidence. However, achieving financial independence requires deliberate planning, discipline, and a long-term perspective.

The journey towards financial independence encompasses various key elements, each playing a crucial role in building a solid foundation for a financially secure future. Let's delve into some of the fundamental principles and strategies involved in working towards financial independence.

1.1 Understand your Financial Goals

Understanding your financial goals is a pivotal step towards building a secure and prosperous financial future. Financial goals serve as a roadmap, guiding your decisions, and helping you prioritize your resources to achieve desired outcomes. This process requires a thoughtful and strategic approach, enabling you to align your aspirations with your financial capabilities and timeframes effectively.

To begin, take the time to assess your current financial situation. Evaluate your income, expenses, assets, and liabilities. This comprehensive overview will provide a clear understanding of your financial standing and help you identify areas that require improvement or adjustment.

Next, define your short-term, medium-term, and long-term financial goals. Short-term goals may include building an emergency fund, paying off high-interest debts, or saving for a specific purchase. Medium-term goals could involve buying a home, funding education, or investing in a business venture. Long-term goals encompass retirement planning, wealth accumulation, and legacy planning.

Quantify your financial goals with specific, measurable, achievable, relevant, and time-bound (SMART) criteria. Assigning a dollar value and a realistic timeline to each goal will serve as a concrete target, providing motivation and direction.

Consider your risk tolerance and investment preferences when setting financial goals. Some individuals may prefer conservative investments with lower potential returns but minimal risk, while others may be comfortable with higher-risk investments offering potentially greater rewards.

Review your financial goals periodically and make necessary adjustments as circumstances change. Life events, economic fluctuations, or career advancements may influence your goals, necessitating a reassessment of your financial plan.

Develop a comprehensive financial plan that outlines the strategies and steps needed to achieve your goals. This plan may include budgeting, debt management, investment allocation, and tax optimization. Seeking professional financial advice can be valuable in creating a well-informed and tailored plan that suits your individual needs.

Track your progress regularly. Monitoring your financial journey allows you to celebrate achievements, stay motivated, and identify any deviations from your plan. Be prepared to adapt to unforeseen challenges and be flexible in your approach, while remaining committed to your ultimate objectives.

Practice disciplined financial habits. Saving consistently, avoiding unnecessary expenses, and adhering to your financial plan are crucial for successful goal attainment. Developing financial discipline will foster the resilience needed to stay on track during both favorable and challenging economic conditions.

However, keep in mind that financial objectives can change. Since life is dynamic, situations always change. Accept the chance to reevaluate and reset your objectives to keep them in line with your changing aspirations and financial situation.

However, understanding your financial goals is a critical pillar of financial success. By taking a thoughtful and strategic approach, setting specific objectives, and crafting a well-defined plan, you can navigate your financial journey with confidence and clarity. Consistent monitoring, financial discipline, and adaptability will ultimately enable you to attain your financial dreams and build a secure and fulfilling future.

1.2 Establish a Budget

Establishing a budget is a crucial step toward achieving financial independence. A budget serves as a roadmap for your finances, enabling you to control your spending, save for the future, and make informed decisions about your money. By taking charge of your income and expenses, you can create a solid foundation for financial stability and ultimately work towards achieving your long-term goals.

Here are some key steps to consider when establishing a budget:

Assess your current financial situation: Begin by examining your income, expenses, debts, and savings. This evaluation will provide a clear picture of your financial standing and help identify areas for improvement.

Decide what you want to accomplish financially and set financial goals. Whether it's paying off debt, saving for a down payment on a house, or building an emergency fund, establishing clear goals will give your budget a purpose and motivate you to stick to it.

Track your income and expenses: Monitor your income sources and carefully track your expenses. This will allow you to understand where your money is going and identify any unnecessary or excessive spending.

Categorize your expenses: Divide your expenses into categories such as housing, transportation, groceries, utilities, entertainment, and so on. This categorization helps you understand your spending patterns and identify areas where you can potentially cut back.

Differentiate between needs and wants: Distinguish between necessities (needs) and discretionary expenditures (wants) by separating out your spending. Prioritize your needs and allocate a reasonable portion of your income to wants while ensuring your needs are met.

Create a budget plan: Based on your income, expenses, and goals, establish a budget plan that outlines how you will allocate your money. Assign specific amounts to each category, ensuring that your income covers all your expenses while leaving room for savings and debt repayment.

Save and invest: Allocate a portion of your income toward savings and investments.

Create an emergency fund that can pay for three to six months of costs. Consider long-term investments like retirement accounts or other investment vehicles that align with your financial goals.

Regularly review and adjust your budget: Financial circumstances can change over time. It's essential to regularly review your budget, assess your progress, and make adjustments as needed. This flexibility allows you to adapt to new circumstances and stay on track.

Seek professional advice if needed: If you're struggling to establish a budget or have complex financial situations, don't hesitate to seek guidance from a financial advisor. They can provide personalized advice, help you create a realistic budget, and offer strategies to achieve your financial independence faster.

Do not forget that creating a budget is a continuous process. It requires ongoing effort and discipline. By consistently following your budget and making wise financial choices, you can take control of your money, reduce stress, and work towards achieving financial independence.

1.3 Cut Back on Expenses

In the face of ever-increasing living costs, economic uncertainty, and changing financial priorities, effectively managing personal expenses has become a crucial aspect of financial well-being. Cutting back on expenses is an essential step towards achieving financial stability, ensuring the ability to save for future goals, and creating a safety net for unexpected events. You can judiciously cut back on expenses without compromising your overall quality of life.

Firstly, before embarking on any expense-cutting journey, it is imperative to conduct a detailed analysis of your current spending patterns. Create a comprehensive budget that includes all essential and discretionary expenses. Track your spending for at least a month, using budgeting apps or spreadsheets to gain a clear understanding of where your money is going. Identifying areas where you overspend and recognizing unnecessary expenses will pave the way for informed decision-making.

Also, trim monthly subscriptions and memberships. In today's digital age, subscriptions and memberships have become ubiquitous, and their cumulative costs can be surprisingly high. Evaluate all the subscriptions you currently hold, including streaming services, gym memberships, magazine subscriptions, etc. Consider whether each one brings significant value to your life and cancel any that you rarely use or can live without. Opting for more cost-effective plans or sharing subscriptions with family or friends can also help reduce expenses.

Furthermore, adopt energy-efficient practices. Energy consumption can substantially impact monthly expenses. Implement energy-efficient practices in your household, such as using LED bulbs, turning off lights and appliances when not in use, maintaining HVAC systems regularly, and insulating your home. These simple changes can lead to significant savings on utility bills over time.

Additionally, never forget to optimize transportation costs, it can be a major expense for many individuals. Explore cost-effective alternatives, such as carpooling, using public transportation, biking, or walking when possible. Additionally, consider downsizing to a more fuel-efficient vehicle or evaluating whether car ownership is necessary if public transport can meet your needs.

Next, grocery expenses often constitute a significant portion of monthly budgets. Adopt savvy shopping habits by making lists before going to the store, comparing prices, buying in bulk for non-perishable items, and using coupons or reward programs to your advantage. Planning meals ahead of time can also reduce food waste and save money.

Going forward, high-interest debts, such as credit cards and personal loans, can weigh heavily on your finances. Explore opportunities to refinance or consolidate debts to secure lower interest rates and better terms. By reducing interest payments, you can allocate more money towards savings or paying off debt faster.

Nonetheless, it is important to negotiate and seek discounts. When it comes to recurring expenses, negotiating with service providers or companies can lead to cost reductions. This includes negotiating lower interest rates on loans, seeking better insurance premiums, or haggling with utility providers. Additionally, actively seek out discounts, promotions, and loyalty rewards for everyday purchases to lower costs.

However, cutting back on expenses requires discipline, commitment, and a proactive approach to personal finance. By conducting a thorough expense analysis, distinguishing between needs and wants, and making strategic choices to optimize various aspects of daily life, you can achieve financial stability, reduce financial stress, and work towards their long-term financial goals. Embracing these strategies will empower you to make informed decisions that align with your values and aspirations, ensuring a brighter and more secure financial future.

1.4 Invest for the Future

Investing for the future is a critical aspect of personal finance that involves allocating resources, such as money, time, or effort, with the aim of generating returns and building long-term financial security. Whether you're planning for retirement, funding your children's education, or achieving financial independence, investing wisely can significantly impact your future financial well-being. We will provide essential insights into the key concepts, strategies, and considerations involved in investing for the future.

First and foremost, you need to understand **the Importance of Investing** as it is essential for:

- Wealth Accumulation: Through investing, you can grow your savings and assets, generating additional income over time.
- Inflation Protection: Investing helps combat the eroding effects of inflation, preserving your purchasing power.
- Long-Term Goals: Investing enables you to achieve financial goals like retirement, buying a home, or starting a business.

Also, know **the key Concepts of Investing**, which are:

- Risk and Return: Investments typically involve a trade-off between risk and potential return. Generally, higher-risk investments have the potential for greater returns, but they also carry a higher chance of losing money.

- Diversification: Spreading your investments across different asset classes, such as stocks, bonds, real estate, and commodities, reduces risk and enhances potential returns.

- Compound Growth: The power of compounding allows your investments to grow exponentially over time, as both the initial investment and the accumulated returns generate further gains.

- Time Horizon: Your investment time horizon (short-term, medium-term, or long-term) influences the type of assets you should consider and the level of risk you can tolerate.

Moving forward, get to know **the investment vehicles**, which are:

- Stocks: Owning shares of a company makes you a partial owner, and their value can increase over time, providing capital appreciation and sometimes dividends.
- Bonds: Bonds are debt securities where investors lend money to an entity (government or corporation) and receive periodic interest payments along with the principal amount upon maturity.
- Real Estate: Investing in real estate properties can offer rental income,

potential appreciation, and tax benefits.

- Mutual Funds and ETFs: These pooled investment vehicles offer diversification and professional management, allowing investors to access various assets with ease.
- Retirement Accounts: Retirement-specific accounts like 401(k)s or IRAs often offer tax advantages to encourage long-term savings.

Nevertheless, **Create an Investment Strategy**:

- Define Goals: Set clear and realistic financial goals based on your needs, time horizon, and risk tolerance.
- Risk Assessment: Understand your risk tolerance and invest accordingly. Younger investors can generally

afford to take on more risk, while those closer to retirement may prefer more conservative investments.

- Asset Allocation: Diversify your portfolio across different asset classes to reduce risk and maximize returns.
- Regular Contributions: Consistent contributions to your investments allow you to benefit from dollar-cost averaging and compound growth.
- Periodic Review: Reevaluate your investment strategy periodically to ensure it aligns with your changing goals and market conditions.

Get acquainted with **the mitigating Risks**, which are:

- Emergency Fund: Before investing, establish an emergency fund to cover unexpected expenses and avoid the need to liquidate investments during downturns.

- Insurance: Adequate insurance coverage, such as health, life, and property insurance, safeguards your financial well-being in the face of unforeseen events.
- Avoiding Speculation: Differentiate between investing and speculating. Avoid high-risk, speculative investments with uncertain outcomes.

Investing for the future is a crucial aspect of financial planning and wealth building. By understanding key investment concepts, setting clear goals, diversifying your portfolio, and consistently contributing over time, you can work towards achieving financial security and realizing your long-term aspirations. Remember to review your investment strategy regularly and seek professional advice when needed to make informed decisions and navigate the ever-changing financial landscape. Start early, be disciplined, and let the power of compounding work in your favor to secure a brighter financial future.

1.5 Build an Emergency Fund

An emergency fund acts as a financial safety net, providing you with the means to cover unexpected expenses and cope with unforeseen circumstances without relying on credit cards or loans. It is a fundamental part of any solid financial plan and can prevent you from falling into debt during challenging times. Here's a comprehensive guide on how to build an emergency fund:

Firstly, you need to understand the purpose of an emergency fund: it is meant to cover essential expenses in case of unexpected events like medical emergencies, car repairs, job loss, or any other unforeseen situation. It should not be used for non-urgent expenses like vacations or luxury purchases.

Secondly, set clear financial goals. Determine how much money you want to have in your emergency fund. Three to six months' worth of living expenses should generally be saved. However, the actual amount may vary based on individual circumstances. If you have dependents or work in an industry with uncertain job prospects, you may consider saving more.

Furthermore, you must calculate your living expenses, track your monthly spending to understand your essential living expenses accurately. This includes rent or mortgage, utilities, groceries, insurance, transportation, and any other fixed costs.

Next, start small, but start now. If you don't have an emergency fund yet, don't be discouraged. Begin by setting aside a small portion of your income each month and gradually increase the amount as you become more comfortable with saving.

However, create a separate account, open a savings account specifically for your emergency fund. Keeping it separate from your regular checking or savings account will make it less tempting to dip into for non-urgent expenses.

Nonetheless, automate your savings, set up an automatic transfer from your checking account to your emergency fund every time you receive your paycheck. In this manner, you'll automatically save money on a regular basis.

Don't forget, whenever you receive unexpected money, like a tax refund, bonus, or gift, consider putting a portion of it into your emergency fund to give it a boost.

It is also important to re-evaluate your fund regularly. As your financial situation changes, reassess the amount you need in your emergency fund. Major life events like marriage, having children, or changing jobs can impact the size of your fund.

Going forward, avoiding risky investments is crucial. Your emergency fund is not meant to be invested in stocks, mutual funds, or other high-risk assets. Keep it in a low-risk, easily accessible account like a savings account or a money market fund.

Also, developing an emergency fund necessitates self-control and perseverance. Stay committed to your savings goal, even when it feels challenging or slow progress.

Lastly, use your emergency fund wisely. When a genuine emergency arises, such as unexpected medical bills or a job loss, use your emergency fund wisely. Once you've utilized it, focus on replenishing it as soon as possible.

Remember, building an emergency fund is not a one-time task but an ongoing process.

It may take time to reach your desired savings goal, but having an emergency fund in place will provide you with peace of mind and financial security when you need it the most.

1.6 Begin a Side Hustle

In today's dynamic and ever-changing economic landscape, the concept of a traditional 9-to-5 job has evolved. More and more individuals are embracing the idea of starting a side hustle, a part-time venture that allows them to explore their passions, diversify their income streams, and gain financial independence. Whether it's pursuing a creative outlet, capitalizing on specialized skills, or turning a hobby into a profitable venture, a side hustle can be a rewarding and fulfilling endeavor. This guide aims to provide a comprehensive roadmap for aspiring entrepreneurs on how to begin their side hustle journey with confidence and success.

• The first crucial step in starting a side hustle is to define your objectives and passions. Reflect on your interests, skills, and hobbies that could potentially be monetized. Identify what excites you the most and aligns with your long-term aspirations. Setting clear goals will not only help you stay focused but will also ensure that your side hustle remains enjoyable and sustainable.

• Conduct thorough research and market analysis to understand your target audience, competitors, and potential demand for your product or service. Identify gaps in the market that your side hustle can address uniquely. This will help you tailor your offerings to meet specific customer needs and stand out from the competition.

• A well-structured business plan is essential for any entrepreneurial endeavor, including a side hustle. Outline your mission, vision, and the strategies you will employ to achieve your goals. Include a financial plan, budgeting for initial expenses, revenue projections, and marketing strategies. Having a solid business plan will provide a roadmap for your actions and serve as a reference point throughout your side hustle journey.

• Effective time management is necessary to juggle a side business with your primary work or other obligations. Create a schedule that allows you to dedicate sufficient time to your side hustle without compromising your primary commitments. Set reasonable timelines, order projects by importance, and refrain from taking on too much. Consistency and discipline are key to making progress and growing your side hustle steadily.

• In today's digital era, establishing an online presence is critical for reaching a wider audience and increasing your side hustle's visibility. Create a professional website or online store to showcase your products or services. Leverage social media platforms to engage with potential customers and build a loyal following. Quality content and meaningful interactions are vital for cultivating a strong online brand.

• As you launch your side hustle, be prepared to test and refine your offerings based on customer feedback. Encourage customers to provide honest reviews and use their input to improve your products or services continuously. Flexibility and a willingness to adapt are essential traits for any successful entrepreneur.

• Ensure that you keep a close eye on your side hustle's financial health. Separate personal and business finances to maintain clarity and track expenses accurately. Invest in cost-effective marketing strategies and prioritize reinvesting profits into growing your side hustle. If required, think about asking financial professionals for guidance.

Beginning a side hustle can be an exciting and rewarding venture. If you follow these steps and stay committed to your goals, you can navigate the challenges and enjoy the journey of entrepreneurship. Remember that success may take time, but with perseverance, passion, and continuous improvement, your side hustle can flourish into a thriving business that complements your career and brings you personal and financial fulfillment.

1.7 Concentrate on Getting Rich and Wealthy

In today's fast-paced and competitive world, the pursuit of financial prosperity has become a primary goal for many individuals. The desire to achieve wealth and abundance is not merely about amassing material possessions, but it encompasses a broader aspiration for financial security, freedom, and the ability to live life on one's own terms. Concentrating on getting rich and wealthy is a multifaceted journey that involves not only financial acumen but also self-discipline, perseverance, and a growth mindset. Let's delve into the importance of focusing on building wealth, the various dimensions of wealth, and the strategies to achieve financial success.

Understanding the Importance of Wealth: Wealth is not synonymous with greed or avarice; rather, it is a means to fulfill one's dreams, aspirations, and responsibilities. It offers the freedom to make choices that enrich life experiences, contribute to society, and create a positive impact. Furthermore, financial stability allows individuals to cope with unexpected challenges, emergencies, and provides a buffer against economic uncertainties. By concentrating on getting rich and wealthy, individuals can attain a state of financial security that positively influences their overall well-being and mental peace.

Dimensions of Wealth: Wealth is not limited to monetary riches alone; it encompasses a range of dimensions that contribute to a fulfilling life. These dimensions include financial wealth, physical health, emotional well-being, strong relationships, intellectual growth, and a sense of purpose. Concentrating on getting rich should not be limited to monetary goals, but it should strive for a holistic balance that enhances all aspects of life. Achieving wealth in these diverse dimensions creates a more profound and lasting sense of contentment and accomplishment.

Cultivating a Wealth Mindset: Concentrating on getting rich necessitates the development of a wealth mindset. This mindset involves adopting positive attitudes towards money, abundance, and opportunities. A wealth mindset acknowledges the importance of financial education, ongoing learning, and the willingness to take calculated risks. It involves embracing challenges and failures as learning opportunities, rather than setbacks, and maintaining a sense of perseverance even in the face of obstacles. Cultivating a wealth mindset empowers individuals to leverage their talents, skills, and resources effectively to achieve financial goals.

Strategic Financial Planning: A crucial aspect of concentrating on getting rich involves strategic financial planning. This involves setting clear financial goals, creating a budget, managing debt, and making informed investment decisions. Diversifying investments and understanding the principle of compounding helps to grow wealth steadily over time. Additionally, seeking advice from financial experts and staying abreast of market trends can enhance financial decision-making. Moreover, focusing on generating multiple streams of income can increase the potential for wealth accumulation.

Aligning with Purpose and Passion: Getting rich is not just about amassing wealth for its own sake; it is about aligning one's financial pursuits with personal passions and purpose. Pursuing avenues that resonate with one's interests and skills leads to a more fulfilling journey towards wealth. When financial goals align with one's purpose, the motivation to succeed becomes intrinsic, and the path to wealth becomes more enjoyable. This alignment also fosters a sense of contribution and meaning, as wealth can be utilized to support causes that matter and positively impact the world.

Therefore, Concentrating on getting rich and wealthy is a multifaceted endeavor that goes beyond the pursuit of material possessions. It involves understanding the importance of wealth, embracing a holistic perspective of wealth dimensions, cultivating a wealth mindset, engaging in strategic financial planning, and aligning financial pursuits with passion and purpose. By adopting these principles, you can embark on a fulfilling journey towards financial prosperity, enabling you to lead more enriched and meaningful lives while making a positive impact on society.

Remember, the pursuit of wealth is not solely about the destination but the transformation that occurs along the way.

Working towards financial independence is a journey that requires dedication, discipline, and informed decision-making. It is a goal that many aspire to achieve, and rightfully so, as it offers numerous benefits and opportunities for a secure and fulfilling life.

To attain financial independence, it is crucial to cultivate good financial habits, such as budgeting, saving, and investing wisely. Staying informed about personal finance and seeking professional advice when necessary can help navigate the complexities of money management effectively.

Remember that financial independence is not a one-size-fits-all concept. It can mean different things to different people, and the path to achieving it may vary. Whether it involves paying off debts, building multiple streams of income, or early retirement, defining your own version of financial independence is essential.

Throughout the journey, setbacks and challenges are inevitable, but perseverance and a long-term outlook are key. Celebrate every milestone achieved, no matter how small, and learn from any financial mistakes along the way.

Ultimately, the pursuit of financial independence should be balanced with enjoying life in the present and nurturing meaningful relationships. Strive for a harmonious balance between financial security and personal fulfillment.

With dedication, knowledge, and a clear vision, working towards financial independence is an attainable goal that can pave the way for a more empowered and prosperous future. So, take charge of your financial well-being today and set yourself on the path towards a more fulfilling and abundant life.

Chapter 2: Avoid Porn

In our ever-connected world, the internet has become an indispensable tool, reshaping the way we learn, communicate, and explore our interests. However, as technology advances, so do the challenges it presents. One of the most pervasive issues of our digital age is the easy accessibility of explicit content, commonly referred to as pornography. While the debate surrounding its ethical implications continues, there is a growing consensus about the potential harm it can cause to individuals and society at large.

This chapter is an essential mantra that resonates with those seeking empowerment and wellness amid the digital deluge. It goes beyond merely denouncing pornography and instead calls for a more comprehensive understanding of the multifaceted impact it can have on individuals and relationships. We will explore the reasons to avoid pornography, the potential consequences of its consumption, and strategies to foster a healthier digital lifestyle.

2.1 Understand the Dangers of Porn

While pornography, or "porn," is a complex and controversial thing to talk about, there is a growing body of evidence suggesting that excessive consumption of pornography can lead to various negative consequences, both for individuals and society as a whole. Let's explore the dangers of porn, including its potential impacts on mental health, relationships, sexuality, and societal implications.

Impact on Mental Health:

- Addiction: One of the primary concerns with pornography is its addictive nature. Similar to other addictive behaviors, excessive porn consumption can lead to compulsive and problematic patterns, making it difficult for individuals to control their urges to view explicit content.

- Desensitization: Frequent exposure to explicit sexual content may lead to desensitization, where individuals become less sensitive to the emotional aspects of sexual relationships. This could result in difficulties forming intimate connections and experiencing genuine emotions in real-life sexual encounters.

- Anxiety and Depression: Some studies suggest a link between excessive porn consumption and increased levels of anxiety and depression. This association may be attributed to feelings of guilt, shame, or dissatisfaction related to porn use or difficulties in interpersonal relationships due to unrealistic expectations set by pornography.

Impact on Relationships:

- Distorted Expectations: Pornography often portrays unrealistic and idealized sexual encounters. As a result, consumers may develop unrealistic expectations about their own and their partner's bodies, performance, and preferences. This can lead to dissatisfaction in real-life sexual relationships and intimacy issues.

- Infidelity and Relationship Dissatisfaction: Research has shown that excessive porn consumption may increase the likelihood of infidelity or create dissatisfaction within existing relationships. Consuming pornographic content may create a sense of emotional disconnection from one's partner and lead to seeking alternative sources of sexual satisfaction.

- Communication Breakdown: In some cases, porn use can lead to communication breakdown between partners, as discussing feelings or concerns related to porn consumption can be challenging or embarrassing.

Impact on Sexuality:

- Objectification of Sexuality: Pornography often objectifies individuals, reducing them to mere objects of sexual pleasure. This can influence how consumers perceive and interact with others in real-life, leading to a distorted view of sexuality and consent.

- Inhibition of Intimacy: Overconsumption of porn can inhibit individuals' ability to experience true intimacy, emotional connection, and vulnerability in sexual relationships. This could lead to difficulties forming meaningful connections with others.

- Escapism: Pornography can serve as a form of escapism for some individuals, using it to cope with stress, anxiety, or emotional challenges. Over reliance on porn as a coping mechanism may prevent individuals from addressing underlying issues in a healthy way.

Societal Implications:

- Violence and Coercion: Some studies suggest that exposure to violent or coercive themes in pornography can influence attitudes towards violence, consent, and gender roles. This can contribute to a more accepting or desensitized attitude towards harmful behavior.

- Exploitation and Trafficking: The pornography industry has faced ongoing concerns regarding the exploitation of performers and potential links to human trafficking. Supporting unethical or non-consensual content indirectly contributes to these issues.

Impact on Adolescents: Young people are particularly vulnerable to the negative effects of pornography due to their developing brains and limited sexual education. Early exposure to explicit content can influence their attitudes towards sex, relationships, and body image.

Ethical Concerns:

- Consent and Exploitation: The ethics of pornography consumption are a contentious issue. Critics argue that much of the content is produced under exploitative conditions, and consumers may unwittingly support unethical practices by consuming such content.

- Privacy and Revenge Porn: The distribution of non-consensual explicit content (revenge porn) can have severe emotional and psychological consequences for the victims, leading to cyberbullying, harassment, and damage to personal and professional lives.

Seeking a Balanced Approach:

It is essential to promote a balanced approach towards sexuality and porn consumption, which includes:

- Sexual Education: Comprehensive sex education is crucial in teaching individuals about consent, healthy relationships, and the potential risks associated with porn.
- Communication: Encouraging open and honest communication about sexual preferences, desires, and

boundaries within intimate relationships.

- Support and Therapy: For those struggling with pornography addiction or related issues, seeking support from therapists, counselors, or support groups can be beneficial.

Understanding the dangers of porn is essential for fostering healthier attitudes towards sexuality, relationships, and personal well-being. While not everyone who consumes porn will experience negative consequences, it is crucial to be aware of the potential risks and to approach its consumption with moderation, critical thinking, and consideration for ethical concerns.

2.2 Recognize the Signs of Addiction

Pornography addiction, like any other form of addiction, can have a significant impact on an individual's life and relationships. It is essential to recognize the signs of porn addiction early on to seek appropriate help and support. Some typical warning indicators and symptoms include the following:

One significant sign is **compulsive behavior.** One of the most apparent signs of porn addiction is the inability to control the urge to watch pornographic content. Addicted individuals may find themselves repeatedly seeking out explicit materials, even when they had initially intended not to do so.

Another sign is **escalating use.** Over time, those struggling with porn addiction may need more explicit or hardcore content to achieve the same level of arousal or satisfaction. This escalation can lead to a cycle of increasing consumption that becomes challenging to break.

Next is **neglecting responsibilities.** A person with porn addiction might neglect their responsibilities, such as work, school, household chores, or social obligations, in favor of spending more time viewing pornography.

Next is **disturbed sleep patterns.** Excessive consumption of pornography can lead to disrupted sleep patterns. Addicted individuals may stay up late into the night watching explicit content, which can result in fatigue and decreased productivity during the day.

Relationship issues are another sign. Porn addiction can strain personal relationships. The addicted person may become emotionally distant, have difficulties with intimacy, or struggle to maintain a healthy sexual relationship with their partner.

You may also experience **decreased interest in other activities.** As the addiction takes hold, you may lose interest in hobbies, sports, or other activities you once enjoyed. Pornography becomes your primary source of pleasure and occupies most of your time.

Feelings of guilt and shame is another one. Porn addiction often leads to feelings of guilt and shame. You may realize that your behavior is harmful but feels unable to stop, leading to a cycle of self-loathing and secrecy.

Here is another - **withdrawal symptoms.** When you or someone addicted to porn try to stop or cut back, you may experience withdrawal symptoms such as irritability, anxiety, or restlessness.

Another relevant sign is **hiding behavior.** Porn addicts often go to great lengths to hide their activities from others. They may clear browsing history, use incognito mode, or create secret accounts to keep their behavior concealed.

Nevertheless, **decline in mental health** is also experienced. Prolonged exposure to pornography can lead to a decline in mental health, including depression, anxiety, or feelings of inadequacy.

If you or someone you know exhibits several of these signs, it is crucial to seek help from a mental health professional or addiction counselor. Porn addiction can have serious consequences on a person's well-being and relationships, and early intervention can greatly improve the chances of recovery. Remember, addiction is a treatable condition, and seeking help is a sign of strength, not weakness.

2.3 Break the Cycle of Porn Addiction

Breaking the cycle of porn addiction is crucial for leading a healthy, fulfilling life. This addiction can have severe consequences on one's mental, emotional, and physical well-being. By overcoming this habit, you can regain control of your life and experience a multitude of positive benefits.

Firstly, breaking free from porn addiction will significantly improve your mental health. Pornography can lead to distorted views of relationships and intimacy, contributing to feelings of loneliness, anxiety, and depression. By killing its impact, you can develop authentic associations with others and cultivate better confidence.

Secondly, breaking the cycle of porn addiction allows you to reclaim your time and productivity. Pornography can be a time-consuming habit that interferes with daily responsibilities, work, and personal goals. By breaking free from its grip, you can channel your energy into more meaningful pursuits, hobbies, and passions. Moreover, overcoming porn addiction can lead to a heightened sense of self-control and discipline. Conquering any addiction requires commitment and resilience, and the journey of recovery can strengthen your willpower. This newfound discipline will positively impact other aspects of your life, empowering you to make better choices in various situations.

Additionally, breaking free from porn addiction can greatly improve your intimate relationships. Pornography can create unrealistic expectations and comparisons, leading to dissatisfaction with real-life partners. By abandoning these artificial fantasies, you can foster deeper connections and intimacy in your relationships, leading to greater overall satisfaction.

Furthermore, the physical benefits of overcoming porn addiction should not be overlooked. Frequent exposure to explicit content can disrupt normal brain chemistry, potentially leading to issues like erectile dysfunction. By breaking the cycle, you can restore your brain's natural responses and experience improved sexual health.

So, how do you break the cycle of porn addiction? It can be challenging, but it's possible with determination and support.

Here are a few stages you can consider:

- **Acknowledge the problem:** Recognize that you have a porn addiction and accept that you need to make a change.
- **Seek support:** Reach out to friends, family, or a therapist who can offer understanding and encouragement throughout the process.
- **Identify triggers:** Identify situations or emotions that lead you to watch porn and find healthy alternatives to cope with them.

- **Set boundaries:** Establish clear boundaries for internet use and develop a plan to avoid triggering content.

- **Engage in healthy activities:** Find new hobbies, exercise, meditate, or participate in social activities to occupy your time and energy positively.

- **Install filters and blockers:** Consider using software or apps that block access to explicit content to reduce temptation.

- **Join support gatherings:** Interface with other people who are confronting comparative difficulties to share encounters and methodologies.

- **Practice self-compassion:** Be patient with yourself and don't be too hard on yourself if you slip up. Recovery is a process.

- **Focus on personal growth:** Work on improving other aspects of your life, like relationships, career, or education.
- **Celebrate progress:** Acknowledge and celebrate each step you take towards overcoming your addiction.

Then, by taking the brave step to break the cycle of porn addiction, you set a positive example for others who may be struggling with similar challenges. Your journey of recovery can inspire and support those seeking to overcome their own addictions, fostering a sense of community and understanding.

2.4 Find Healthy Alternatives to Porn

Finding healthy alternatives to porn is crucial for those seeking to reduce or eliminate their reliance on explicit content and promote a healthier, more balanced lifestyle. While it is essential to acknowledge that individual experiences with porn can vary greatly, some individuals may find that porn consumption negatively impacts their mental health, relationships, and overall well-being. Fortunately, there are numerous constructive and positive alternatives to consider.

First is to **cultivate real relationships**: One of the most potent alternatives to porn is investing time and energy into building real and meaningful relationships. Spending quality time with friends, family, or a partner can foster a sense of connection and intimacy that may not be fulfilled through pornographic content.

Secondly, **engage in physical activities**: Exercise and physical activities provide a healthy way to release endorphins and reduce stress, which can be an effective way to counteract the urge to turn to porn. Regular exercise also promotes body confidence and self-esteem.

Third is to **pursue hobbies and interests**: Dedicating time to hobbies or passions can be a fulfilling alternative to porn. Engaging in creative pursuits, such as writing, painting, playing an instrument, or crafting, allows individuals to channel their energy into productive and gratifying activities.

Next, **practice mindfulness and meditation**: Mindfulness practices can help individuals become more aware of their impulses and reactions. Meditation and mindfulness techniques can provide a sense of inner peace and self-awareness, reducing the likelihood of turning to porn as a coping mechanism.

Furthermore, **educate yourself**: Instead of consuming explicit content, consider engaging in educational materials related to human relationships, intimacy, and sexual health. Understanding these topics can lead to healthier perceptions of intimacy and sexuality.

Going forward, **seek professional support**: For those who find it challenging to break away from porn addiction, seeking support from a therapist, counselor, or support group can be invaluable. Professionals can provide personalized guidance to address underlying issues and implement healthy coping strategies.

Nevertheless, **embrace self-care practices**: Taking care of oneself holistically is essential in maintaining emotional well-being. Engaging in self-care activities, such as journaling, taking relaxing baths, or practicing aromatherapy, can help individuals cope with stress and emotional challenges without turning to porn.

You have to **limit access to pornographic content**: Practicing self-discipline is crucial. Limiting access to pornographic content by blocking websites or removing explicit content from devices can help reduce temptation.

Then, **foster emotional intimacy**: Building emotional intimacy with a partner involves open communication, vulnerability, and trust. Engaging in meaningful conversations and connecting on an emotional level can help strengthen the bond between partners and diminish the need for external stimulation like porn.

Next thing to do is to **explore healthy sexual expression**: Exploring consensual and healthy sexual experiences with a partner can help fulfill sexual needs in a positive and satisfying way. Open communication about desires and boundaries is key to fostering a supportive and gratifying sexual relationship.

Know that each individual's journey to finding healthy alternatives to porn will be unique. It's essential to be patient with oneself and seek support when needed. Breaking away from porn may take time, but with determination, self-awareness, and a focus on healthier alternatives, individuals can foster a more fulfilling and balanced lifestyle.

2.5 Unfollow Half-naked Girls

Avoiding porn and maintaining a healthy digital environment is an important concern for many individuals. Unfollowing half-naked girls or any sexually explicit content can indeed be an effective strategy to reduce exposure to pornographic material. This approach aims to create a safer online experience by eliminating triggers and temptations that may lead to the consumption of explicit content.

Pornography addiction is a real and widespread issue, affecting people of all ages and backgrounds. It can lead to negative consequences in various aspects of life, including relationships, mental health, and personal development. Consequently, individuals seeking to break free from this addiction often explore different strategies to prevent relapses and maintain self-control.

Unfollowing half-naked girls is a proactive step that addresses the issue of sexual content appearing on social media feeds. Many social media platforms have algorithms that analyze user preferences and present content that aligns with those interests. If someone has previously engaged with or searched for sexualized content, they might unknowingly be exposed to explicit material on their feed.

By actively unfollowing accounts or pages that frequently post sexualized images, individuals can create a safer digital space for themselves. This process involves reflecting on one's values and consciously choosing not to endorse or engage with content that objectifies individuals or perpetuates harmful attitudes towards sexuality.

Furthermore, unfollowing sexually explicit content can also serve as a psychological barrier against falling back into old habits. When individuals make a conscious effort to remove such content from their feeds, they reaffirm their commitment to abstain from pornography and reinforce their willpower. This act of intentional self-regulation can empower individuals to take control of their digital consumption and foster a healthier relationship with technology.

However, it is essential to recognize that unfollowing half-naked girls alone may not be sufficient to address the root causes of pornography addiction. Addressing underlying psychological issues, seeking professional help, and finding healthy coping mechanisms are equally crucial in the journey to recovery.

Remember, breaking free from pornography addiction is a challenging process that requires dedication, patience, and support. Unfollowing half-naked girls is just one part of a comprehensive strategy to create a healthier digital environment and promote personal growth and well-being. By adopting multiple strategies and seeking help when needed, individuals can build resilience and reclaim control over their lives.

2.6 Go on a Date

Going on a date is a positive and healthy way to redirect one's focus away from pornography and build more meaningful connections with others. Engaging in social activities, like dating, can help individuals create deeper emotional connections and reduce the temptation to turn to porn for instant gratification.

Dating allows people to experience genuine human interaction, fostering communication skills, empathy, and understanding. It provides an opportunity to learn about someone else's interests, values, and aspirations, which can be far more rewarding and fulfilling than the superficial experiences often associated with pornography.

Moreover, dating encourages self-improvement and personal growth. When preparing for a date, individuals may focus on grooming, dressing well, and building their self-confidence, leading to enhanced self-esteem and a positive self-image. These improvements can help one break free from the negative cycle of porn consumption and instead focus on becoming a better version of themselves.

Going on a date also offers a chance to explore shared hobbies and interests. Engaging in activities together, such as going to a museum, trying out a new restaurant, or attending a live performance, can strengthen the bond between two people and contribute to a more satisfying and wholesome connection.

Furthermore, dating allows individuals to develop a sense of emotional intimacy, which is often missing in the context of pornography. Sharing feelings, thoughts, and vulnerabilities with a partner fosters trust and a deeper understanding of one another, leading to a healthier and more meaningful relationship.

It is essential to approach dating with genuine intentions and respect for the other person. Being honest and open about one's past struggles, including pornography use, can create a foundation of trust and openness in the relationship. If a partner is understanding and supportive, they can become an invaluable ally in overcoming challenges related to pornography.

However, it's important to recognize that dating alone may not be a complete solution to overcoming pornography addiction or the temptation to view explicit content. Seeking professional help, such as therapy or support groups, can be beneficial in addressing the underlying issues and developing healthier coping mechanisms.

Going on a date is a significant step toward avoiding pornography and fostering more meaningful connections with others. It offers opportunities for personal growth, emotional intimacy, and shared experiences that can contribute to a more fulfilling and balanced life. Combining dating with appropriate support and self-awareness can lead to positive changes in one's life and help break free from the negative impacts of pornography.

2.7 Manage Your Urges

Managing urges to avoid pornography is an essential aspect of maintaining a healthy and balanced lifestyle. Pornography addiction can have detrimental effects on mental health, relationships, and overall well-being. Here are some strategies to help manage urges effectively:

- Recognize and acknowledge the urges when they arise. Avoid suppressing or ignoring them, as this can lead to increased anxiety and tension. By acknowledging the urges, you can work towards understanding their triggers and patterns.

- Analyze the situations, emotions, or activities that trigger the urge to watch pornography. Common triggers may include stress, loneliness, boredom, or certain environments. Once identified, take proactive steps to address or avoid these triggers.

- Incorporate healthy habits into your daily routine, such as regular exercise, sufficient sleep, and a balanced diet. Engaging in physical activities can help reduce stress and provide alternative ways to channel energy.

- Create a support system, surround yourself with supportive and understanding individuals who can offer encouragement and help you stay accountable in your efforts to overcome urges.

- Find alternative activities, redirect your focus towards constructive and engaging activities when faced with urges. Consider hobbies, socializing, reading, or pursuing personal interests to divert your attention away from pornography.

- Implement technology barriers, use tools such as website blockers, content filters, or parental controls to limit access to explicit content online. These measures can act as an extra layer of protection against impulsive urges.

- Be patient and persistent, breaking free from pornography addiction takes time and effort. Be patient with yourself and be aware that setbacks can happen. Stay persistent in your commitment to change and focus on long-term recovery.

Know that managing urges is an ongoing process, and it's normal to face challenges along the way. The key is to be proactive, compassionate towards yourself, and stay committed to your journey towards a healthier and porn-free life.

In the pursuit of personal growth and maintaining healthy relationships, we must take an unwavering stance to avoid the alluring yet detrimental grasp of pornography. Let us break free from its captivating allure and reclaim our inner strength, unlocking the boundless potential that lies within. Embrace the beauty of authentic connections, where love, respect, and intimacy flourish. By avoiding porn, we forge a path towards self-discovery, emotional fulfillment, and true empowerment. Together, let's embark on this transformative journey, liberating our minds and hearts from the chains of illusion, and embracing a life of purpose, passion, and genuine fulfillment. Remember, the power to shape our destinies lies in our hands, and by making this conscious choice, we lay the foundation for a brighter and more meaningful future.

Chapter 3: Read Everyday

In a fast-paced and technology-driven world, the habit of reading every day holds the key to unlocking a treasure trove of knowledge, creativity, and personal growth. From captivating novels that transport us to distant lands to informative non-fiction books that expand our horizons, the act of reading is a gateway to a realm of endless possibilities.

Embracing the habit of reading daily goes beyond the acquisition of information; it cultivates a sense of empathy as we immerse ourselves in the lives and experiences of characters, both fictional and real. By engaging with diverse perspectives, we can develop a deeper understanding of the world around us and foster a more compassionate society.

Moreover, reading every day stimulates the mind, enhancing cognitive abilities and critical thinking skills. As we explore different genres, our imagination blossoms, allowing us to envision innovative solutions and creative pathways in our own lives. The written word has the power to inspire, challenge, and motivate us to embark on exciting journeys of self-discovery.

Beyond the confines of traditional books, the digital age has broadened the scope of reading. Articles, blogs, and other online content offer a vast array of topics to explore, catering to individual interests and preferences. Reading online also encourages participation and engagement with a global community of readers, making the experience more interactive and socially enriching.

In this chapter, we will delve into the importance of cultivating the habit of reading every day and explore the myriad of benefits it brings to our personal and intellectual growth. Whether one reads for pleasure, knowledge, or personal development, embracing the written word as a daily ritual can positively shape our lives and unlock the limitless potential of our minds. So, let us embark on this literary journey and discover the wonders that lie between the pages, one day at a time.

3.1 The Benefits of Reading Everyday

Reading every day offers numerous benefits that can transform your life. Firstly, it enhances your knowledge, expanding your horizons beyond imagination. By delving into diverse subjects, you develop a deeper understanding of the world and become more empathetic towards others.

Secondly, reading sharpens your cognitive abilities, boosting memory, focus, and analytical skills. It exercises your brain, helping you stay mentally agile and reducing the risk of cognitive decline as you age.

Moreover, regular reading improves your vocabulary and communication skills, making you more articulate and persuasive in conversations and writing. It empowers you to express your thoughts effectively, leaving a lasting impact on others.

In addition, reading is a fantastic stress-reliever and a gateway to relaxation. Engaging with a captivating book allows you to escape the stresses of daily life and unwind in a world of imagination.

Furthermore, it fosters creativity and critical thinking, inspiring you to explore new ideas and think outside the box. As you immerse yourself in various narratives, you'll find yourself approaching challenges with a fresh perspective.

Nonetheless, reading enhances emotional intelligence, as you empathize with characters' experiences and learn valuable life lessons from their journeys. It cultivates empathy, compassion, and emotional awareness, enriching your relationships with others.

So, reading every day is a powerful habit that enriches your mind, hones your skills, and enhances your overall well-being. Embrace the world of books, and you'll discover a boundless source of wisdom and inspiration that can truly change your life for the better.

3.2 How to Find Time to Read Everyday

Finding time to read every day can be challenging, but with a few adjustments to your daily routine, it's definitely achievable. Here are some tips to help you incorporate reading into your daily schedule:

Set a Specific Time: Choose a specific time each day dedicated to reading, such as during your morning coffee, lunch break, or before bedtime. Incorporate reading into your daily schedule. Consistency will make it easier to form a reading habit.

Utilize Idle Time: Take advantage of idle moments throughout the day, like commuting, waiting in line, or during breaks, to read a few pages or articles on your phone or e-reader.

Create a Reading Space: Designate a cozy and comfortable reading nook at home or work where you can relax and immerse yourself in your book.

Limit Screen Time: Reduce time spent on social media or watching TV to free up more time for reading. Use apps or website blockers if necessary to avoid distractions.

Start Small: If you're struggling to find time, begin with short reading sessions, like 10-15 minutes per day, and gradually increase the duration as you become more comfortable with the habit.

Carry a Book Everywhere: Keep a book with you at all times or use reading apps on your phone to capitalize on unexpected downtime.

Utilize Audiobooks and Podcasts: When you can't physically read, listen to audiobooks or educational podcasts during activities like exercising or doing household chores.

Set Reading Goals: Determine how much time you can realistically devote to reading each day. Start with a few minutes and gradually increase it as the habit strengthens. Set achievable reading goals, whether it's a certain number of books per month or finishing a specific book within a week. This will help you stay focused and committed.

- **Prioritize Reading:** Make reading a priority in your daily to-do list. Consider it a crucial component of your self-care routine.

Multitask Wisely: Combine reading with other activities, like listening to audiobooks while doing household chores or exercising.

Set Reading Alarms: Set reminders on your phone or use reading apps that send notifications to prompt you to read at designated times.

Remember, finding time to read is about making reading a priority in your life. By incorporating these smart strategies, you can cultivate a daily reading habit that enhances your knowledge and brings joy to your life.

3.3 Find Books That You Enjoy

In the vast literary landscape, finding books that genuinely resonate with your interests, preferences, and emotions can be a rewarding yet challenging pursuit. The journey to uncovering literary gems that ignite enjoyment requires a thoughtful approach, as individual tastes and inclinations vary significantly. In the end, you will be equipped with practical strategies and valuable insights to facilitate the process of discovering books that captivate, inspire, and bring genuine pleasure to your reading experience.

The first step in finding books that evoke enjoyment is gaining a clear understanding of your personal preferences. Reflecting on past reading experiences, genres, and themes that have sparked interest is an invaluable starting point. By identifying specific elements that have resonated with you in the past, a clearer picture of your literary tastes emerges, paving the way for targeted book exploration.

Secondly, diversifying reading choices can broaden the horizons of enjoyment. While having preferred genres is natural, exploring different literary categories exposes you to unique perspectives, writing styles, and narrative structures. Engaging with diverse genres fosters a more comprehensive appreciation for the art of storytelling and increases the likelihood of stumbling upon unexpected treasures.

Also, in a world filled with an overwhelming number of book choices, seeking recommendations from fellow readers, book clubs, or reputable book review platforms can streamline the search for enjoyable reads. Word-of-mouth suggestions and trusted literary sources can introduce you to hidden literary gems that might have otherwise eluded your attention.

Moreover, leveraging technology and online tools can significantly aid in finding books tailored to your preferences. Platforms offering personalized book recommendations based on past reading habits, user ratings, and thematic analyses provide valuable assistance in uncovering books that align with your interests.

Furthermore, before committing to a book, sampling excerpts or reading reviews can offer valuable insights into the writing style, narrative tone, and plot dynamics. By gaining a glimpse of the author's storytelling prowess, you can make more informed decisions about which books are likely to resonate with you, ultimately enhancing the potential for enjoyment.

Next, in the pursuit of finding enjoyable books, embracing serendipity plays an essential role. Sometimes, wandering into a bookstore and perusing shelves at random or selecting a book based solely on its cover can lead to delightful literary surprises. Allowing for spontaneous encounters with new authors and stories can be a rewarding aspect of the reading journey.

So, discovering books that evoke genuine enjoyment is an enriching experience that aligns intimately with personal preferences and interests. By understanding individual tastes, embracing diversity, seeking recommendations, utilizing technology, and embracing the element of serendipity, you can navigate the vast literary landscape more effectively, ensuring a fulfilling and enjoyable reading experience that resonates on a profound level.

3.4 Start a Book Club or Online Reading Group

Book clubs and online reading communities have become increasingly popular in recent years, offering avid readers a fantastic platform to connect, discuss, and share their love for literature. Both options, joining a physical book club or participating in an online reading community, come with their unique advantages and provide enriching experiences for bibliophiles. Let's delve into the benefits and features of each:

Physical book clubs provide a social and interactive experience where you can discuss literature with like-minded individuals, gaining different perspectives and insights. This fosters a sense of community, promotes lively discussions, and encourages you to explore books you might not have chosen otherwise.

Also, physical book clubs often host regular meetings, enabling members to engage in meaningful conversations about the chosen book, literary themes, characters, and plotlines. This social aspect adds an enjoyable dimension to the reading experience.

Furthermore, book clubs often feature a variety of genres and authors, exposing members to books they might not have chosen themselves. This diversity broadens their literary horizons and encourages exploration beyond their comfort zones.

On the other hand, online reading allows for greater flexibility and convenience. One of the significant advantages of online reading communities is their global reach. Readers from all over the world can participate, fostering diverse perspectives and cultural exchange.

Online reading community also offers convenience and flexibility, as members can participate from the comfort of their homes, at any time that suits their schedule. This is particularly beneficial for busy individuals or those with limited access to physical book clubs.

Online community often provides access to digital libraries, e-books, and audiobooks, making it easier for members to access a vast array of literary works without physical limitations.

Engaging with an online reading community can also give you the opportunity to write and share book reviews, helping others discover new books and authors.

Both physical book clubs and online reading communities share common benefits:

Stimulating Discussions: Engaging with others who have read the same book sparks thought-provoking discussions, encouraging deeper analysis and interpretations.

Accountability: Being part of a reading group instills a sense of commitment to finish assigned books, ensuring participants stay on track with their reading goals.

Shared Interests: Book clubs foster connections between individuals with similar interests, creating a sense of belonging and shared passion for literature.

Personal Growth: Through active participation in discussions, members develop critical thinking and communication skills, enhancing their understanding of the literary world.

Ultimately, the choice depends on your preferences and lifestyle - whether you choose to join a physical book club or engage in an online reading community, both options offer incredible opportunities for personal growth, social interaction, and an enriched reading experience. So, find the community that aligns with your interests and preferences. Remember, the key to a successful book club or online reading community experience is active participation, openness to new ideas, and a willingness to engage with others in a constructive manner.

3.5 Use Technology to Make Reading Easier

This has been a game-changer for many people as it opens up new possibilities and improvises accessibility. Here are some important factors to talk about:

Digital Books and E-Readers: E-books have revolutionized the way we consume written content. With e-readers and mobile devices, users can access a vast library of books at their fingertips, adjust font size, background color, and use text-to-speech features for enhanced reading experiences.

Text-to-Speech (TTS): TTS technology allows the conversion of written text into spoken words, enabling those with visual impairments or learning disabilities to access and comprehend written content more easily.

Audiobooks and Podcasts: Audiobooks provide an alternative to traditional reading, allowing people to listen to books while on the go, which is beneficial for those with busy schedules or visual impairments.

Language Translation Tools: Technology facilitates easy access to books and articles in different languages. Translation tools and apps help readers overcome language barriers, promoting cross-cultural understanding.

Reading Assistance Software: Various software tools, such as Read&Write, provide support to struggling readers by offering features like word prediction, dictionary integration, and highlighting text to aid comprehension.

Digital Libraries and Online Resources: The internet offers a wealth of reading materials, including articles, research papers, and educational content, making it convenient to find information on virtually any topic.

Social Reading Platforms: Technology has enabled social reading experiences, where readers can interact, discuss, and share their thoughts on books and articles, fostering a sense of community and enhancing the reading process.

Accessible Formats: Technology has made it possible to create books in accessible formats like Braille and large print, ensuring that individuals with visual impairments can enjoy a wider range of reading materials.

Interactive and Multimedia Elements: E-books can incorporate interactive features, such as quizzes, videos, and animations, making the reading experience engaging and informative, especially for children and students.

Smart Learning Algorithms: Personalized reading recommendations and adaptive learning platforms utilize AI algorithms to suggest content tailored to individual interests and reading levels, encouraging continuous learning.

While technology has significantly improved reading accessibility and convenience, it is essential to consider potential challenges, such as digital distractions and the digital divide, ensuring that technology remains a tool to enhance reading rather than hinder it. Continuous efforts in refining and expanding these technologies will pave the way for an even more inclusive and enriched reading experience for people worldwide.

3.6 Make Reading a Part of Your Daily Routine

Incorporating reading into your daily routine is a transformative habit that can enrich your life in numerous ways. Whether you are an avid reader or someone looking to cultivate a reading habit, the benefits are undeniable.

Firstly, reading expands your knowledge and understanding of the world. Through books, you can explore different cultures, historical events, and diverse perspectives. This exposure broadens your horizons and fosters empathy and compassion for others.

Moreover, reading is an excellent way to enhance your cognitive abilities. Regular reading sharpens your critical thinking, problem-solving skills, and vocabulary. It also improves focus and concentration, which can be beneficial in all aspects of life, from work to leisure activities.

Reading also acts as a stress-reliever and helps in relaxation. Engaging with a captivating story can transport you to another world, offering an escape from daily pressures. This mental respite is essential for maintaining balance and emotional well-being.

Furthermore, reading fosters creativity and imagination. As you immerse yourself in various narratives, you develop the ability to envision alternative scenarios and think outside the box. This creative thinking can be advantageous in both personal and professional endeavors.

Nonetheless, reading can significantly improve your communication skills. Exposure to different writing styles and language usage expands your linguistic abilities, making you a more articulate and effective communicator.

To incorporate reading into your daily routine, start with a manageable goal, such as reading for 15-30 minutes each day. Set aside a specific time, whether it's in the morning with a cup of coffee or before bedtime. Choose genres that genuinely interest you, and gradually expand your reading repertoire.

Note, like any habit, consistency is key. Make reading a pleasurable and rewarding experience, and you'll soon find it an indispensable part of your daily life. So, take the first step towards a more enriching and fulfilling life by making reading a part of your daily routine.

3.7 Build a Personal Library

Building a personal library is an enriching journey that opens doors to new worlds and ideas. By curating a collection of books, you're investing in your knowledge, imagination, and personal growth. Each book becomes a treasure, offering insights, solace, and inspiration whenever you delve into its pages. Here's a comprehensive guide to help you get started and make the most of your personal library:

Define Your Purpose, determine the purpose of your personal library. Is it for leisure reading, self-improvement, academic pursuits, or a mix of everything? This clarity will guide your book selection process.

Set Realistic Goals, building a library takes time and effort. Start with a manageable number of books and set achievable goals for expanding your collection.

Choose Diverse Subjects, and don't limit yourself to just one genre. Embrace diversity by including fiction, non-fiction, biographies, history, science, philosophy, and more. A wide range of subjects will keep your reading experience exciting and enlightening.

Choose Quality over Quantity. Focus on acquiring well-written and thought-provoking books. Opt for editions with good print quality and durable bindings, as they'll stand the test of time.

Explore local bookstores and libraries to browse and discover new titles. Engaging with physical books can be a delightful experience and may lead to serendipitous finds.

Utilize online platforms to discover and purchase books. E-books and audiobooks are also great alternatives, especially when space is limited.

Designate a cozy reading nook in your home where you can immerse yourself in the world of books. A comfortable chair, good lighting, and a bookshelf nearby create the perfect ambiance.

Organize your collection systematically by author, genre, or any other method that suits you. Consider using book cataloging apps to keep track of your books and maintain a digital library.

Engage with your books actively by taking notes, highlighting passages, and jotting down reflections. This personalizes your reading experience and enhances understanding.

Share your love for books with friends, family, or join book clubs to discuss literature. Engaging in meaningful discussions about books can deepen your understanding and appreciation of the material.

Don't forget to include books by local authors or lesser-known writers. Supporting emerging talent can be immensely gratifying.

Revisiting books you've read in the past allows you to gain new insights and perspectives as you evolve as a person.

Remember, there's no rush—take your time, explore diverse genres, and embrace the joy of discovering hidden gems. Your library will be a reflection of your unique interests and passions, making it a source of comfort and empowerment. Embrace this journey with enthusiasm, and your personal library will become a treasured sanctuary of knowledge and inspiration.

It is evident that the simple act of reading every day has the potential to transform lives and shape a brighter future. Reading is more than simply a leisure activity; it's a doorway to knowledge, creativity, and self-improvement. Through the pages of books, we venture into uncharted territories, explore different cultures, and gain profound insights into the human experience.

By committing to reading every day, we cultivate a habit that not only broadens our horizons but also strengthens our cognitive abilities. Like a muscle that becomes more robust with consistent exercise, our minds become sharper and more agile with each literary encounter. The power of reading extends far beyond the confines of entertainment; it nurtures critical thinking, empathy, and creativity, equipping us with the tools to navigate the complexities of life.

The journey of reading every day is one of profound transformation and self-discovery. It empowers us with knowledge, enriches our minds, and opens our hearts to the vastness of the human experience. It is a lifelong adventure, an endless exploration of worlds both real and imaginary, and a key to unlocking the potential within ourselves. So let us embrace the power of reading, turning the pages of books with curiosity and wonder, and let it illuminate our path towards a brighter and more enlightened future.

Chapter 4: Workout

Working out, a fundamental aspect of leading a healthy and fulfilling life, involves engaging in various physical activities to improve overall fitness and well-being. From cardiovascular exercises like running, cycling, and swimming, to strength training, flexibility exercises, and mindfulness practices like yoga, working out encompasses a broad range of activities catering to diverse fitness goals.

The benefits of working out are vast and encompass both physical and mental aspects. Regular physical activity helps maintain a healthy weight, build strength and endurance, enhance flexibility, and improve cardiovascular health. It can also boost energy levels, promote better sleep, and reduce the risk of chronic illnesses such as heart disease, diabetes, and certain types of cancer.

Beyond the physical advantages, working out positively impacts mental health. Exercise releases endorphins, the body's natural feel-good chemicals, which can alleviate stress, anxiety, and depression, promoting a sense of well-being and happiness. Additionally, engaging in workouts provides an opportunity for personal growth, discipline, and self-motivation.

One of the most attractive aspects of working out is its versatility. Whether an individual prefers solo activities like running or group exercises like dance classes, there is a workout style to suit every personality and preference. Additionally, advancements in technology have led to the proliferation of fitness apps and wearable devices, enabling people to track their progress, set goals, and receive personalized training plans.

Working out can be a social and communal experience as well, with many gyms, fitness centers, and sports clubs offering group classes or team-based activities. This fosters a sense of community and support, making the fitness journey more enjoyable and motivating.

To maximize the benefits of working out and avoid potential injuries, it's essential to start with proper warm-ups, maintain correct form during exercises, and listen to the body's signals. Consulting with a fitness professional or healthcare provider before embarking on a new workout routine is always a wise decision, especially for individuals with pre-existing health conditions.

So, working out is a dynamic and essential practice that empowers individuals to achieve their fitness goals, enhances their physical and mental well-being, and fosters a vibrant and active lifestyle. Regardless of age, background, or fitness level, incorporating regular exercise into one's routine can lead to a more fulfilling and spectacular life.

4.1 The Importance of Exercising Regularly

Regular exercise is crucial for maintaining healthy physical and mental health. It plays a vital role in enhancing various aspects of our well-being and significantly contributes to a higher quality of life. Here are some of the key reasons why exercising regularly is so important:

Physical Health: Regular exercise helps in improving cardiovascular health, reducing the risk of heart diseases, stroke, and high blood pressure. It strengthens muscles, bones, and joints, reducing the likelihood of injuries and osteoporosis. Physical activity also aids in maintaining a healthy weight, which is essential for preventing obesity-related conditions.

Mental Health: Exercise is not only beneficial for the body but also for the mind. Endorphins, sometimes known as "feel-good" hormones, which are released as a result of it might lessen tension, anxiety, and despair. Regular physical activity can enhance mood, boost self-esteem, and improve cognitive function.

Weight management: Regular exercise aids in calorie burning and the maintenance of a healthy weight. Combining exercise with a balanced diet is an effective approach to managing weight and preventing weight-related health issues.

Increased Energy: Regular physical activity helps fight weariness by boosting energy levels. It improves blood flow and oxygen supply to the muscles and organs, enhancing overall vitality and endurance.

Better Sleep: People who exercise regularly tend to experience improved sleep patterns and better sleep quality. The importance of getting a good night's sleep for overall health and wellbeing.

Disease Prevention: Regular exercise can reduce the risk of developing chronic diseases such as type 2 diabetes, certain types of cancer, and metabolic syndrome. It also helps in managing existing conditions more effectively.

Social Interaction: Participating in group exercises or sports can provide opportunities for social interaction and foster a sense of community, which is beneficial for mental health.

Brain Health: Exercise has been linked to improved cognitive function and a reduced risk of cognitive decline as we age. Memory, focus, and general brain function can all be improved by it.

Stress Reduction: Physical activity is an effective way to relieve stress and tension. Engaging in exercise helps to clear the mind and offers a healthy outlet to cope with life's challenges.

Longevity: According to studies, people who exercise frequently have longer, healthier lives than people who adopt sedentary lifestyles.

To reap the benefits of regular exercise, it's essential to find activities that you enjoy and can sustain in the long term. Whether it's going for a brisk walk, jogging, cycling, swimming, dancing, or participating in team sports, finding something you love will make it easier to stay motivated and committed to a regular exercise routine.

It's crucial to consult with a healthcare professional before starting any new exercise regimen, especially if you have pre-existing health conditions or concerns. They can provide personalized advice and recommendations tailored to your specific needs and fitness goals. Remember that consistency is key, and even small amounts of daily physical activity can make a significant difference in your overall health and well-being. So, get moving and make exercise an integral part of your life!

4.2 Find a Workout Routine that Works for You

The quest for a workout routine that suits an individual's specific needs and goals is crucial for achieving optimal fitness results. With an array of exercise regimens available, finding the right one can be overwhelming. However, by understanding key considerations, personalized preferences, and fitness objectives, individuals can embark on a journey towards identifying a workout routine that not only works but also ensures long-term adherence and success.

- The first step in discovering a suitable workout routine is to clearly define and prioritize personal fitness objectives. Whether the aim is to build muscle, enhance cardiovascular endurance, lose weight, or simply improve overall health, understanding these goals is essential. Each objective requires specific exercise modalities, intensities, and time frames to achieve the desired outcomes effectively.

- Considering individual preferences is a crucial aspect of creating a sustainable workout routine. Some individuals may prefer the camaraderie of group classes, while others may find solace in solitary workouts. Similarly, determining whether outdoor or indoor exercises are more appealing can significantly impact adherence to the chosen routine. By aligning preferences with exercise choices, individuals are more likely to stay committed and motivated.

- An effective workout routine should strike a balance between cardiovascular and strength training exercises. Cardiovascular workouts, such as running, cycling, or swimming, help improve heart health and burn calories. On the other hand, strength training, through weightlifting or bodyweight exercises, enhances muscle strength and promotes a leaner physique. Combining both types of workouts ensures a holistic approach to overall fitness.

- An essential aspect of any workout routine is the principle of progressive overload. This concept involves gradually increasing the intensity, duration, or frequency of exercises over time to challenge the body and promote continuous adaptation. By implementing progressive overload safely and effectively, individuals can avoid plateaus and continually progress towards their fitness goals.

- A well-rounded workout routine should incorporate flexibility exercises and prioritized recovery days. Stretching and mobility work enhance joint flexibility, reduce the risk of injuries, and aid in post-workout recovery. Adequate rest between intense workouts allows the body to repair and rebuild, preventing burnout and ensuring sustainable progress.

- For those seeking a more tailored and expertly-designed workout routine, consulting a certified fitness trainer or exercise specialist can be invaluable. These professionals can assess individual needs, provide personalized recommendations, and ensure that workouts are performed correctly and safely.

Finding a workout routine that works for an individual involves a thoughtful process of aligning fitness goals, preferences, and exercise modalities. By combining cardiovascular and strength training exercises, incorporating progressive overload and recovery, and seeking professional guidance when necessary, individuals can discover a personalized workout routine that promotes lasting fitness achievements and overall well-being. Remember that consistency, dedication, and self-awareness are essential elements that underpin success on the journey to a healthier and more active lifestyle.

4.3 Create a Gym-free Workout Routine

Creating a gym-free workout routine can be a great way to stay active and fit without the need for expensive gym memberships or equipment. It offers flexibility, convenience, and the opportunity to exercise in the comfort of your own space.

To design an effective gym-free workout routine, consider the following elements:

Goal Setting: Define your fitness goals to tailor the routine accordingly. Whether it's improving strength, endurance, flexibility, or overall health, having clear objectives will help you stay focused and motivated.

Bodyweight Exercises: Bodyweight exercises are essential for a gym-free routine since they utilize your own body weight as resistance. Include exercises like push-ups, squats, lunges, planks, and burpees to target various muscle groups.

Cardiovascular Exercises: To improve cardiovascular health, incorporate exercises like running, jogging, jumping jacks, high knees, and mountain climbers into your routine. You can do these activities outdoors or inside if you have enough space.

HIIT (High-Intensity Interval Training): HIIT is an excellent way to burn calories and improve overall fitness in a short amount of time. Combine bursts of intense exercise with short periods of rest to maximize the effectiveness of your workouts.

Yoga and Stretching: Don't forget the importance of flexibility and relaxation. Include yoga or stretching exercises to improve flexibility, balance, and reduce the risk of injury.

Resistance Bands and Dumbbells: If you're willing to invest in some minimal equipment, resistance bands and dumbbells can add variety and intensity to your workouts. They are relatively affordable and easy to store.

Circuit Training: Design circuit workouts that target different muscle groups. Move from one exercise to another with minimal rest to keep your heart rate up and challenge your muscles.

Online Resources and Apps: Take advantage of the plethora of workout routines available online or through fitness apps. Many platforms offer guided workout sessions, timers, and tracking tools.

Consistency and Progression: Consistency is key to seeing results. Gradually increase the intensity and complexity of your workouts to avoid plateaus and keep making progress.

Rest and Recovery: Allow your body sufficient time to recover after intense workouts. Overtraining can lead to injuries and burnout, so listen to your body and take rest days when needed.

Monitor Your Progress: Keep track of your workouts, sets, and reps to track your progress over time. Seeing improvements can be incredibly motivating.

Remember to warm up before each session and cool down afterward to prevent injuries and optimize your performance. Always consult a healthcare professional before starting any new exercise routine, especially if you have pre-existing health conditions or concerns.

With dedication, creativity, and consistency, you can design an effective and enjoyable gym-free workout routine that will help you achieve your fitness goals.

4.4 Incorporate Fitness into Your Daily Routine

Incorporating fitness into your daily routine is not just a way to stay physically healthy, but it also brings numerous benefits to your overall well-being. By making exercise a regular part of your day, you're setting yourself up for success in both your personal and professional life.

First and foremost, regular physical activity enhances your energy levels and boosts productivity. Starting your day with a workout or a brisk walk can invigorate your mind and prepare you to tackle the challenges ahead. Increased energy and focus translate into better performance at work or school.

Moreover, incorporating fitness into your daily routine promotes mental clarity and reduces stress. Exercise triggers the release of endorphins, the feel-good chemicals in your brain, which can help alleviate anxiety and lift your mood. This, in turn, fosters a positive outlook and enhances your ability to handle stress effectively.

Maintaining a consistent exercise routine also improves your overall health, reducing the risk of various chronic diseases such as heart disease, diabetes, and obesity. Regular physical activity strengthens your cardiovascular system, improves lung function, and helps control blood pressure, leading to a healthier and longer life.

Ideally, engaging in fitness activities can be a great way to socialize and build connections with like-minded individuals. Whether it's joining a fitness class, participating in group sports, or going for a run with friends, exercising together can create a sense of camaraderie and support.

Furthermore, integrating fitness into your daily routine sets an excellent example for those around you, especially family and friends. By prioritizing your health, you inspire others to do the same, creating a positive ripple effect within your community.

So, incorporating fitness into your daily routine offers a multitude of benefits. From increased energy and productivity to improved mental well-being and reduced health risks, it's a powerful investment in your long-term happiness and success. So take that first step today, and commit to making fitness an integral part of your life. Your body and mind will thank you, and you'll reap the rewards for years to come.

4.5 The Mind-Body Connection: The Benefits of Exercising for Mental Health

Physical exercise offers numerous benefits for mental health and has been widely recognized as an integral component of a holistic approach to promoting psychological well-being. Engaging in regular exercise can have profound positive effects on various aspects of mental health, enhancing mood, reducing stress and anxiety, improving cognitive function, and fostering overall psychological resilience.

First and foremost, exercise has been shown to stimulate the release of endorphins, commonly referred to as the "feel-good" hormones, which can uplift one's mood and create a sense of euphoria. This natural mood enhancement can help alleviate symptoms of depression and anxiety, providing individuals with a more positive outlook on life.

Moreover, physical activity acts as a powerful stress-reliever. By engaging in exercise, individuals can reduce cortisol levels, the hormone associated with stress, and promote relaxation. Regular physical activity can serve as a healthy coping mechanism, helping individuals manage the challenges and pressures of daily life, ultimately leading to a calmer and more balanced mental state.

In addition to its immediate effects, exercise plays a pivotal role in the long-term management of mental health conditions. Studies have demonstrated that individuals who engage in regular physical activity are less likely to develop certain mental disorders, such as depression and anxiety. Furthermore, exercise has been shown to complement traditional therapeutic interventions, potentially augmenting the efficacy of treatments for individuals already experiencing mental health issues.

Cognitive benefits also accompany a physically active lifestyle. Regular exercise has been associated with improved memory, enhanced concentration, and increased creativity. This heightened cognitive function can lead to improved performance in various tasks, including academic and professional pursuits.

Furthermore, exercise provides a valuable opportunity for social interaction and engagement, fostering a sense of belonging and community. Group activities or sports can help reduce feelings of loneliness and isolation, contributing to enhanced mental well-being and overall life satisfaction.

It is essential to highlight that the benefits of exercise for mental health are not exclusive to rigorous workouts or high-intensity activities. Even moderate exercise, such as walking, yoga, or gardening, can have a significant positive impact on mental well-being. The key is consistency and finding enjoyable physical activities that align with individual preferences and capabilities.

So, the evidence supporting the advantages of exercise for mental health is compelling. Incorporating regular physical activity into one's lifestyle can result in improved mood, reduced stress and anxiety, enhanced cognitive function, and greater psychological resilience. As an accessible and cost-effective intervention, exercise remains a fundamental tool in promoting mental well-being and should be embraced as a vital aspect of overall health and happiness.

4.6 Stay Motivated to Exercise

It's not always easy to stay motivated to exercise, but it's so important for our physical and mental health. Here are some tips for staying motivated to exercise:

Having specific goals, such as losing weight or running a 5K, can help you stay motivated and focused, so, set specific goals.

Having someone to exercise with can make it more fun and help you stay accountable. Have a workout buddy.

Avoid monotony by trying different exercises and workouts. Variety keeps things fresh and prevents boredom. Try something new to keep things interesting. Mix it up.

Another tip is to make your workout routine enjoyable. Choose exercises that you genuinely enjoy doing. Whether it's dancing, hiking, swimming, or playing sports, doing what you love makes it easier to stay motivated.

Don't be too hard on yourself if you miss a workout or face setbacks. Be Kind to yourself. Acknowledge your efforts and keep moving forward.

Imagine yourself reaching your fitness goals and the positive impact it will have on your life. Visualizing success can boost motivation.

However, remember to listen to your body and don't overdo it. Exercise should feel challenging but not painful. If you feel pain, stop and consult a doctor.

4.7 Fit Exercise into a Busy Schedule

It can be tough to find time to exercise when you have a busy schedule, but it's important to make it a priority. That notwithstanding, these tips can help you fit exercise into a busy schedule:

- Wake up early. Set your alarm for 30 minutes earlier than usual and use that time to squeeze in a quick workout before your day begins.

- Take advantage of lunch breaks. If you have a lunch break, use it to go for a walk or do a quick workout at home or in the office.

- Use your commute time. If you take public transportation, get off a stop early and walk the rest of the way. Or, if you drive, park further away from your destination and walk the extra distance. You could also try squeezing in mini-workouts throughout the day, like doing squats while you brush your teeth or taking the stairs instead of the elevator.

- Consider multi-tasking by doing strength training while you watch TV or listen to music.

- Combine social time with exercise time. Instead of meeting friends for coffee or drinks, suggest a walk or jog in the park. You can also find a workout buddy who has similar goals and schedules. Working out with someone else can make it more fun and help keep you accountable.

- And don't forget about technology. There are lots of apps and online videos that make it easy to fit in a workout, even when you're short on time.

- Take advantage of your weekends. Plan a family outing like a hike or a bike ride. Even a day of yard work can count as exercise.

- Make exercise part of your daily routine. Just like you brush your teeth or eat breakfast every day, try to make exercise a habit. It doesn't have to be a long workout - even 10 minutes a day is better than nothing.

- Try a standing desk. Sitting all day is bad for your health, so try a standing desk or a walking treadmill desk. You can get your work done while you burn calories. And finally, remember to take care of yourself.

- Make sure you're getting enough sleep, drinking enough water, and eating a healthy diet. When you take care of your overall health, it's easier to find time for exercise. Do you have any questions about these tips?

And there you have it, the journey of working out! Remember, every step you take, every sweat you shed, brings you closer to a stronger, healthier version of yourself. Embrace the challenges, celebrate the victories, and never forget that your commitment to fitness goes beyond the gym. So keep pushing, keep lifting, and keep moving forward. Your body will thank you, your mind will thank you, and you'll discover the incredible power that lies within you. Now, go out there and conquer your fitness goals, one rep at a time! Stay motivated, stay inspired, and let the world witness the incredible transformation that comes from the dedication to working out. Cheers to a stronger, happier you!

Chapter 5: Make a Wardrobe

Making a wardrobe is an empowering process that allows you to curate a personal collection of clothing that reflects your style, values, and identity. From carefully curating timeless essentials to expressing your unique identity through fashion, making a wardrobe is more than just assembling clothes – it's an art of self-discovery and empowerment. It involves mindful choices, selecting versatile pieces, and focusing on quality over quantity. By building a wardrobe that suits your lifestyle, you not only save time and money but also contribute to sustainability by reducing fast fashion's impact. Unleash your creativity, embrace versatility, prioritize essential basics, conquer any occasion with a wardrobe that speaks volumes without saying a word, and let your wardrobe become a true reflection of the confident and authentic individual you are.

5.1 Identify Your Personal Style

Identifying your personal style is a fundamental aspect of cultivating a cohesive and authentic wardrobe that reflects your individuality and personality. Discovering it is what makes you feel comfortable, confident, and authentic in your wardrobe choices. Developing a distinctive style not only enhances your confidence but also communicates a powerful visual message to the world.

The first step in this journey is self-discovery. Take time to introspect and understand your preferences, interests, and lifestyle. Consider the colors, patterns, and silhouettes that resonate with you and make you feel most comfortable. Analyze your favorite fashion icons or sources of inspiration to identify common themes in their style that align with your taste.

Next, assess your body shape and proportions to select clothing that flatters your unique figure. Tailored pieces that complement your physique will elevate your overall appearance and create a polished impression.

Building a versatile wardrobe revolves around investing in timeless and high-quality essentials. Classic pieces such as well-tailored blazers, crisp white shirts, well-fitted jeans, and a little black dress serve as the foundation for creating various outfits suitable for different occasions.

Experimentation is vital in the process of discovering your personal style. Don't shy away from trying new styles, patterns, or accessories that catch your eye. Fashion is an evolving art, and allowing yourself to embrace novelty may lead to surprising and delightful discoveries.

Remember, personal style is an ever-evolving expression of self, so be open to adapting and refining it as you grow and change. Stay true to yourself and avoid the temptation to conform to fleeting trends. Instead, focus on curating a wardrobe that resonates with your identity and stands the test of time.

Nevertheless, seek feedback from trusted friends or seek guidance from a professional stylist if you find yourself unsure about certain aspects of your style journey. Their insights and expertise can provide valuable perspectives and steer you towards a more cohesive and authentic representation of yourself through your wardrobe choices.

So, identifying your personal style is a rewarding journey of self-expression and empowerment. Embrace individuality, invest in quality essentials, and remain open to exploring new fashion horizons to curate a wardrobe that speaks volumes about your uniqueness and confidence.

5.2 Build a Wardrobe That Suits Your Lifestyle

Building a wardrobe that suits your lifestyle is an art that combines both self-expression and practicality. It involves mindful selection of clothing pieces that resonate with your personality, while also accommodating the demands of your daily activities. To start, assess your typical routines and occasions you frequently encounter, from work to leisure and special events.

Emphasize quality over quantity, investing in durable and sustainable clothing that stands the test of time. Opting for a capsule wardrobe approach, with fewer but well-chosen pieces, simplifies the daily decision-making process and ensures you always have an outfit that aligns with your lifestyle.

Stay attuned to your evolving needs and embrace change when necessary. As your lifestyle shifts, so too should your wardrobe. Be open to letting go of items that no longer serve a purpose and welcoming new additions that complement your present endeavors.

A crucial aspect of building a wardrobe that suits your lifestyle is understanding your body type and dressing to highlight your strengths. This not only enhances your confidence but also ensures comfort throughout the day, allowing you to focus on your goals without distractions.

Consider the climate and weather conditions in your area to tailor your wardrobe accordingly. Layering options for colder climates or breathable fabrics for warmer regions are essential factors to keep in mind.

Not to forget, building a wardrobe is an ongoing journey, and it's okay to take your time. Gradually refine your collection, staying true to your authentic self and prioritizing items that bring joy and utility to your life.

In all, creating a wardrobe that suits your lifestyle is an intimate expression of self-awareness, practicality, and style. It involves thoughtful curation, embracing versatility, quality, and personal preferences. By approaching it with intention and adaptability, you can fashion a wardrobe that resonates with your unique journey through life.

5.3 Make a Shopping List of Essential Pieces

Creating a well-thought-out shopping list of essential wardrobe pieces is a brilliant way to elevate your style and ensure you have versatile outfits for every occasion. Imagine having a closet filled with timeless classics and trendy staples that effortlessly mix and match, providing endless outfit possibilities.

Begin by considering your lifestyle and daily activities. Tailor your list to include pieces that align with your needs, whether it's office attire, casual wear, or formal events. Building a strong foundation with essential pieces will save you time and money in the long run.

Start with the basics, like I earlier mentioned, a crisp white button-down shirt, well-fitted jeans, and a tailored blazer. These timeless items form the backbone of any wardrobe, offering endless pairing options and easy transitions from day to night.

Next, focus on versatility and comfort. A little black dress is a must-have, as it can be dressed up or down for various occasions. A classic trench coat and a pair of neutral-colored chinos or slacks can effortlessly elevate your style and adapt to changing weather conditions.

Don't forget to invest in quality footwear. A pair of comfortable and stylish sneakers, classic leather loafers, and elegant pumps can take your outfits to the next level, adding both practicality and flair to your ensemble.

Consider the seasons as you build your list. For colder months, a cozy cashmere sweater, a well-insulated winter coat, and a pair of stylish ankle boots are essential. For warmer weather, opt for lightweight fabrics like linen, and include breezy dresses and comfortable sandals.

Accessories are the icing on the cake. A few statement necklaces, a stylish watch, and a versatile handbag can instantly elevate your look and add a touch of personality to your outfits.

Ultimately, the key to creating a compelling shopping list for your wardrobe is to focus on quality, versatility, and timelessness. By thoughtfully curating your collection, you'll have a closet filled with pieces that make you look and feel confident, empowered, and effortlessly chic every day.

5.4 Shop For Versatile, Quality Items

When it comes to shopping for your wardrobe, seeking versatile, quality items is the key to unlocking endless style possibilities. Picture yourself effortlessly mixing and matching pieces, effortlessly transitioning from casual to sophisticated looks, and always feeling confident in your appearance.

Don't be afraid to splurge on quality items, as they tend to last longer and maintain their shape and color over time. Quality fabrics like silk, cashmere, and organic cotton not only feel luxurious against your skin but also ensure durability and longevity in your wardrobe.

Consider neutral colors like navy, black, gray, and white for the foundation of your wardrobe. They effortlessly blend with other colors and patterns, making it easy to create cohesive looks.

Also know that shopping for versatility means opting for items that can be dressed up or down. A fashionable pair of ankle boots may lend a dash of sophistication to a casual ensemble, and a striking necklace can transform a plain shirt into a stylish ensemble.

Lastly, embrace your personal style and select items that resonate with you. Whether you lean towards a bohemian flair, a minimalist aesthetic, or a bold and edgy vibe, choosing pieces that align with your taste will make you feel comfortable and confident in any setting.

By curating a wardrobe filled with versatile, quality items, you'll discover the joy of effortless dressing, expressing your individuality, and making a positive impact on the environment through mindful consumption.

5.5 Create a Capsule Wardrobe

Creating a capsule wardrobe is a popular approach to simplify your closet and streamline your style. It involves curating a collection of essential, versatile, and timeless clothing pieces that can be mixed and matched to create numerous outfits. The goal is to simplify your closet, reduce clutter, and make getting dressed easier.

Here's a guide on how to create your own capsule wardrobe:

Assess your lifestyle: Consider your daily activities, work requirements, and social events. This will help you determine the types of clothing you need in your capsule wardrobe.

Identify core pieces: Choose timeless and classic items that form the foundation of your wardrobe, such as neutral-colored tops, bottoms, and outerwear. These pieces should be versatile and easily combinable.

Select accent pieces: Add a few statement pieces or colorful items to bring some personality and style to your capsule wardrobe. These can be accessories, patterned clothing, or unique pieces that complement the core items.

Stick to a color palette: Choose a cohesive color scheme for your wardrobe to ensure everything can be mixed and matched effortlessly. Neutral colors like black, white, gray, and beige work well, but you can add a few pops of color if you like.

Consider the season: Create separate capsule wardrobes for different seasons, making sure to include appropriate clothing for the weather.

Quality over quantity: Invest in high-quality pieces that will last longer and withstand regular wear. It's better to have a few well-made items than a closet full of cheap, fast-fashion pieces.

Pare down your current wardrobe: Declutter by removing items you no longer wear or need. Donate or sell them to make room for the items you truly love and use.

Organize and rotate: Keep your capsule wardrobe well-organized, and consider rotating seasonal items to keep it fresh and suitable for changing weather.

Embrace versatility: Aim for pieces that can be dressed up or down and work well together, so you can create various outfits from a limited number of items.

Assess and update regularly: Periodically evaluate your capsule wardrobe and make adjustments as needed. This will help ensure it remains functional and reflects your evolving style and lifestyle.

A capsule wardrobe is not about restricting yourself but rather embracing simplicity and thoughtful curation. It allows you to make the most of your clothing while reducing decision fatigue and clutter in your daily life.

5.6 Organize Your Closet for Ease of Use

A clutter-free and well-organized closet not only saves you time when getting ready but also ensures that you can easily find and access your belongings. Here's an extensive guide to help you achieve a well-organized closet:

Begin by decluttering, emptying out your entire closet and sorting through your belongings, and parting with items that no longer serve a purpose. Create three piles: keep, donate/sell, and discard. Be ruthless in your decision-making process. Consider items you haven't worn in the past year or those that no longer fit or are in poor condition.

Categorize your clothing, grouping similar items together to create categories. Common categories include shirts, pants, dresses, shoes, accessories, etc. This step will make it easier to find what you need quickly.

Utilize storage solutions by investing in storage solutions that suit your needs. This might include shelves, hanging organizers, bins, hooks, and shoe racks. To increase storage capacity, make use of vertical space.

Use the same type of hanger for each type of clothing. This creates a uniform look and prevents clothes from slipping off. Consider slim hangers to save space.

Arrange your clothes by color within each category. Adopt a system that resonates with you, whether it's color coding or arranging by function. This not only looks aesthetically pleasing but also makes it easier to locate specific items.

If you don't have much room, think about switching up your clothes every season. Store off-season items in clear plastic bins or vacuum-sealed bags to save space.

Place frequently used items at eye level or within easy reach. Items you rarely wear can be stored on higher shelves or in less accessible areas.

Opt for open shelving or clear storage containers whenever possible. Being able to see your items at a glance reduces the chances of forgetting what you own.

Use hooks or small storage containers to organize accessories like belts, scarves, and jewelry. Drawer dividers can help keep smaller items neat and separated.

Label bins or containers to indicate what's inside. This prevents you from having to rummage through multiple containers to find what you're looking for.

Keep shoes organized with shoe racks or cubbies. If space is limited, consider using vertical shoe organizers that hang behind the closet door.

Place a hamper or basket in your closet for dirty clothes. This prevents them from piling up on the floor and keeps your space tidy.

Regularly set aside time to maintain your organized closet. This involves reevaluating your belongings, putting things back in their designated spots, and making adjustments as your needs change.

As you acquire new items, make it a rule to donate or discard something else. This prevents your closet from becoming cluttered again.

Before purchasing new items, consider whether they truly fit your style and needs. This prevents unnecessary accumulation of items that may later contribute to clutter.

It's important to adapt your system as your needs change and to regularly maintain the organization you've established. A well-organized closet can have a positive impact on your daily life by reducing stress, saving time, and promoting a sense of order in your living space.

5.7 Donate or Sell Unused Items

Donating or selling unused items from your wardrobe is a great way to declutter and make better use of your space. Donating to charities or shelters can help those in need, while selling items online or at consignment stores can earn you some extra money.

So, start by going through your closet and sorting your clothes into three piles: keep, donate, and sell.
For clothes you're keeping, organize them by season, color, or style. Finding what you need when getting dressed in the morning will be simpler as a result.

For clothes you are donating or selling, consider the condition of the items whether they hold sentimental value. No one wants to buy or receive clothes that are stained, ripped, or have missing buttons. Also, consider whether the clothes are in style. It's okay to keep clothes that are timeless, but you may want to donate or sell clothes that are out of style.

Whichever route you choose, it's a win-win – either someone benefits from your items, or you benefit from the extra space and funds.

As you step into your newly curated world of clothing, remember that your wardrobe isn't just a collection of fabric and style – it's a manifestation of your identity, your creativity, and your journey. With each piece carefully chosen, you've crafted a reflection of who you are and who you aspire to be. So, wear your choices with pride, walk with confidence, and let your wardrobe be a testament to the artistry of self-expression. Embrace the power of your style and let it tell the story that only you can share with the world.

Chapter 6: Skin Care

In a world where first impressions matter, the canvas that speaks volumes is often overlooked—the skin. Skin care, an art and science intertwined, is more than just vanity; it's a practice rooted in self-care and well-being. From ancient rituals to modern innovations, the journey of caring for one's skin has evolved into a multi-billion-dollar industry. But beyond the trends and products, the core principle remains steadfast: to nourish and protect the body's largest organ.

This chapter delves into the realms of skin care, exploring the myriad layers that make up its essence. From the basics of cleansing, moisturizing, and sun protection to the complexities of personalized routines and cutting-edge treatments, we'll traverse the spectrum of practices that encompass this intricate discipline. Uncover the secrets of ingredients like hyaluronic acid, retinol, and antioxidants, each with its unique role in achieving radiant and healthy skin.

But skin care goes beyond the surface; it's a dynamic interplay of genetics, lifestyle, and environment. As we delve deeper, we'll unravel the symbiotic relationship between diet, hydration, sleep, and skin health, highlighting how a holistic approach can amplify the benefits of any regimen. We'll also touch on the psychological aspect, exploring how self-confidence and emotional well-being are intrinsically tied to the health of our skin.

In a world saturated with an overwhelming array of products and advice, this chapter serves as a compass, guiding you through the labyrinth of choices and trends. Whether you're a skincare novice or a seasoned aficionado, the journey of skin care is a continuous one—an exploration of self-discovery and self-care that extends far beneath the surface. So, embark on this expedition armed with knowledge, and let your skin tell the story of the care and attention it deserves.

6.1 Understand Your Skin Type

To establish an effective skincare routine that addresses your specific needs, understanding your skin type is essential. Skin type classification typically falls into five categories: normal, oily, dry, combination, and sensitive.

Normal skin exhibits a balanced level of moisture, with a smooth texture and minimal blemishes. It requires maintenance to preserve its equilibrium.

Oily skin tends to produce excess sebum, leading to a shiny appearance and potential acne breakouts. Oil control and regular cleansing are crucial for maintaining its health.

Dry skin lacks sufficient moisture, often resulting in flakiness, tightness, and irritation. Hydration and emollient-rich products are vital to alleviate discomfort.

Combination skin displays a blend of characteristics, with an oily T-zone (forehead, nose, and chin) and drier cheeks.

Tailoring products to different areas can help balance the complexion.

Sensitive skin is prone to reactions such as redness, itching, or burning. It requires gentle, fragrance-free formulations and a patch test before introducing new products.

Understanding your skin type requires self-observation and often benefits from professional assessment by a dermatologist. Identifying your skin's unique characteristics empowers you to curate a skincare regimen that promotes a healthy, radiant complexion.

6.2 Create a Daily Skin Care Routine

Creating a daily skincare routine is essential for maintaining healthy and radiant skin. A well-structured regimen can help address various skin concerns and promote overall skin health. Here's an extensive guide to help you get started:

Cleanse: Use a mild cleanser that is appropriate for your skin type to begin your routine. Cleansing removes dirt, oil, and makeup, preparing your skin for subsequent steps.

Exfoliation: In order to get rid of dead skin cells and encourage cell turnover, exfoliate two to three times per week. Avoid excessive exfoliation, as it can lead to irritation. Choose a chemical exfoliant (like AHAs or BHAs) or a mild physical exfoliant.

Toner: A toner helps balance your skin's pH levels and prepares it for the next steps. Choose toners with calming components that are alcohol-free.

Serum: Serums contain concentrated active ingredients targeting specific skin concerns, such as hydration, brightening, or anti-aging. Apply a suitable serum after cleansing and toning.

Moisturize: Be sure to apply moisturizer even if your skin is greasy. Choose a product that matches your skin type and provides hydration without clogging pores. For daytime, use a moisturizer with SPF to protect against UV rays.

Eye Cream: An eye cream can address concerns like puffiness, dark circles, and fine lines around the delicate eye area. Tap it on softly using your ring finger.

Sunscreen: Wearing sunscreen is non-negotiable. UV radiation can damage skin and speed up the aging process. Use a broad-spectrum sunscreen with at least

SPF 30 every morning, even on overcast days.

Nighttime Routine: Your evening routine might include double cleansing (first to remove makeup, second to cleanse skin), followed by your serum and a slightly richer moisturizer. Nighttime is also ideal for using retinoids, which help with cell turnover and combating signs of aging.

Weekly Treatments: Incorporate weekly treatments like masks or overnight masks, targeting specific concerns such as hydration, brightening, or purifying. Make sure these treatments align with your skin's needs.

Hydration and Diet: Remember that skincare isn't just about external products. Staying hydrated and maintaining a balanced diet rich in antioxidants, vitamins, and healthy fats contributes to your skin's overall health.

Consistency is Key: Consistently following your routine is crucial. Results won't happen overnight; you'll likely start noticing improvements after a few weeks of dedicated care.

Listen to Your Skin: Pay attention to how various products affect your skin's reaction. If something causes irritation or discomfort, discontinue use.

Consult a Professional: Consider seeing a dermatologist if you have particular skin issues or conditions. They can provide personalized recommendations and treatments tailored to your skin's needs.

Adjust with Seasons: Remember that your skin's needs can change with the seasons. Adjust your routine accordingly to address dryness in winter or excess oil production in summer.

Creating a daily skincare routine is an investment in your skin's health and appearance. Tailor the routine to your unique needs, stay consistent, and enjoy the benefits of radiant and well-cared-for skin.

6.3 Choose the Right Skin Care Routine

Choosing the right skincare routine goes beyond vanity; it's an investment in your skin's health and well-being. Your skin, the body's largest organ, requires personalized care that considers factors such as skin type, age, and environmental influences.

The knowledge of understanding your skin type – whether it's oily, dry, combination, or sensitive, forms the foundation of your routine, helping you select products that cater to your specific needs. From cleansers to moisturizers, each product should be chosen with your skin's characteristics in mind.

Consider your age and any concerns you may have, such as acne, fine lines, or hyperpigmentation. This guides you towards active ingredients like retinoids, hyaluronic acid, or vitamin C that address your unique skin challenges.

Environmental factors play a significant role. Your location's climate, pollution levels, and sun exposure influence your skin's requirements. Incorporate sunscreen as a non-negotiable step to protect against premature aging and skin damage.

Routine consistency is key. Patience is paramount, as meaningful results often take time. Avoid frequent changes in products, as this can disrupt your skin's balance. Gradually introduce new items and monitor their effects.

A holistic approach extends to lifestyle choices. A balanced diet, hydration, regular exercise, and sufficient sleep all contribute to glowing skin. Manage stress, as it can manifest on your skin, impacting its appearance.

Also, seek professional guidance when needed. Dermatologists can provide expert insights, addressing concerns beyond what over-the-counter products can achieve. Remember, your skin is unique – embracing a personalized skincare routine nurtures its health, radiance, and your self-confidence.

6.4 Incorporate Sun Protection into Your Routine

Incorporating sun protection into your daily routine is not just a choice, but a vital necessity. The sun's harmful ultraviolet (UV) rays can wreak havoc on your skin, leading to premature aging, sunburn, and worst of all, skin cancer. By making sun protection a habit, you're investing in your long-term health and well-being.

Picture a morning ritual that includes applying sunscreen as seamlessly as brushing your teeth. Just a few minutes of effort can save you years of potential skin damage. Sunscreen acts as a shield against UV rays, safeguarding your skin from harm. It's like an insurance policy for your complexion – a small gesture with significant benefits.

Imagine the confidence of stepping outside without worrying about sunburns or uneven skin tone. Incorporating sun protection means you're taking charge of your skin's health and appearance. Not only will you look better, but you'll also feel better knowing you're proactively preventing damage.

Think about the peace of mind that comes with reducing the risk of skin cancer. The statistics are sobering, but by consistently wearing sunscreen and protective clothing, you're significantly lowering your chances of developing this potentially life-threatening condition.

Why then wait? Make wearing sunscreen a necessity in your daily routine. It's an investment in yourself – a way to prioritize your skin's health and radiance. Whether you're heading out for a jog or just walking to your car, remember that a few seconds of sunscreen application can translate into a lifetime of healthy, beautiful skin. Your future self will thank you for the care and attention you're giving to your skin today.

6.5 Treat Skin Conditions

Treating skin conditions involves a variety of approaches depending on the specific issue. Common treatments include topical creams, ointments, or gels containing active ingredients like corticosteroids, antibiotics, retinoids, or antifungals. In more severe cases, oral medications or phototherapy might be recommended. Following are a few typical skin issues and their remedies:

Acne: Acne is often treated with topical treatments like benzoyl peroxide, salicylic acid, or retinoids. Oral antibiotics or hormonal therapies may be prescribed for more severe cases. In-office treatments like chemical peels, microdermabrasion, or laser therapy can also help.

Eczema: Moisturizers and topical corticosteroids are commonly used to manage eczema flare-ups. For severe cases, doctors may prescribe immunosuppressants or newer biologic medications to reduce inflammation.

Psoriasis: Topical corticosteroids, vitamin D analogs, and retinoids are commonly prescribed for psoriasis. Phototherapy, where the skin is exposed to UVB light, can also be effective. Systemic medications or biologic drugs may be used for more severe cases.

Rosacea: Topical antibiotics, azelaic acid, or metronidazole may be recommended to manage rosacea symptoms. Laser therapy can help reduce visible blood vessels or redness.

Hives: Antihistamines are the primary treatment for hives, helping to reduce itching and inflammation. Identifying and avoiding triggers is also important.

Warts: Over-the-counter treatments with salicylic acid or freezing with liquid nitrogen can be used for common warts. In-office procedures like laser therapy or surgical removal might be necessary for stubborn warts.

Fungal Infections: Antifungal creams, powders, or oral medications are used to treat fungal infections like athlete's foot, ringworm, or yeast infections.

Melasma: Sun protection and topical treatments containing hydroquinone, retinoids, or kojic acid are commonly used to manage melasma. Chemical peels and laser therapy can also help reduce pigmentation.

Contact Dermatitis: Avoiding the irritant or allergen is the primary step. Topical corticosteroids and antihistamines may be used to manage symptoms.

Cold Sores: Antiviral creams or oral medications can help manage cold sore outbreaks. Keeping the area moisturized can also prevent cracking and discomfort.

Don't forget, skin conditions vary widely, and what works for one person may not work for another. It's important to follow your dermatologist's recommendations closely, maintain good skin care practices, and be patient, as improvement may take time. Additionally, lifestyle factors such as a balanced diet, proper hydration, stress management, keeping the skin moisturized, using sunscreen, and avoiding triggers like excessive sun exposure can contribute to overall skin health.

6.6 The Importance of Hydration

Hydration is important for maintaining healthy skin. The skin is the body's largest organ and serves as a protective barrier against external elements. Proper hydration is essential for the skin's overall health and appearance.

When the body is well-hydrated, the skin is better equipped to perform its functions effectively. Hydration helps maintain the skin's elasticity, which prevents it from becoming dry, flaky, and prone to cracking. Dry skin can lead to discomfort and even more serious conditions like eczema and dermatitis.

Adequate hydration also contributes to a natural glow and radiance of the skin. When skin cells are hydrated, they plump up, minimizing the appearance of fine lines and wrinkles. Dehydrated skin can appear dull and lackluster, accentuating signs of aging.

Water plays a pivotal role in detoxification and waste elimination from the body. Proper hydration helps flush out toxins and waste products through sweat and urine, reducing the likelihood of skin issues like acne and breakouts. When toxins accumulate in the body, they can manifest on the skin's surface in the form of blemishes.

Moreover, well-hydrated skin is better equipped to heal and repair itself. It can recover more quickly from wounds, cuts, and irritations. This is particularly important for individuals with sensitive skin or those prone to skin conditions.

Lack of hydration can lead to an impaired skin barrier function. The skin's outermost layer, called the stratum corneum, acts as a barrier that prevents moisture loss and protects against environmental aggressors. When this barrier is compromised due to dehydration, the skin becomes more susceptible to irritation, redness, and inflammation.

Incorporating a proper skincare routine that includes hydrating products can significantly improve the skin's health. Using moisturizers, serums, and other hydrating products helps lock in moisture, ensuring that the skin remains supple and soft. It's important to note that external moisturization should be complemented by internal hydration – drinking an adequate amount of water daily.

So, the importance of hydration for the skin cannot be overstated. Well-hydrated skin is not only more resilient against external stressors but also exhibits a healthier, youthful, and radiant appearance. Remember to maintain a balanced internal and external hydration routine for optimal skin health.

6.7 DIY Skin Care Recipes

Sure, I'd be happy to share some DIY skin care recipes! Keep in mind that individual reactions can vary, so it's a good idea to do a patch test before applying any new concoctions to your entire face. Here are a few recipes for different skin concerns:

Moisturizing Avocado Mask: Mash half a ripe avocado and mix it with a tablespoon of honey and a teaspoon of yogurt. Apply the mixture to your face and leave it on for about 15-20 minutes before rinsing with lukewarm water.

Exfoliating Sugar Scrub: Combine coconut oil and brown sugar in an equal amount. Gently massage the scrub onto your skin in circular motions, then rinse off with water. This helps to remove dead skin cells and leaves your skin smooth.

Brightening Turmeric Face Mask: Mix 1 teaspoon of turmeric powder with 2 tablespoons of yogurt and a teaspoon of honey. Before rinsing, apply the paste to your face and let it sit there for 15 to 20 minutes. Turmeric is known for its brightening properties, but it can stain clothing and surfaces, so be careful.

Acne-Fighting Tea Tree Toner:
Combine 1/4 cup of witch hazel with a few drops of tea tree oil. Apply the mixture to a cotton pad and gently swipe it over your clean face. Tea tree oil has antibacterial properties that can help with acne.

Soothing Oatmeal Bath Soak: Oats should be ground into a fine powder and added to the bathwater. Oats have anti-inflammatory properties that can help calm irritated skin.

Hydrating Aloe Vera Gel: Rose water and aloe vera gel should be combined equally. Apply the mixture to your face for a refreshing and hydrating boost.

Nourishing Coconut Oil Hair Mask:
Warm up a few tablespoons of coconut oil and massage it into your scalp and hair. Before washing it off, let it on for at least 30

minutes or overnight. Coconut oil can aid in strengthening and moisturizing hair.

Cleansing Green Tea Steam: Brew a pot of green tea and let it cool slightly. Lean your face over the steam for a few minutes to open up pores and cleanse your skin.

Keep in mind that every person has unique skin, so what works for one person may not work for another. Always do a patch test and introduce new ingredients slowly to avoid adverse reactions. If you have any allergies or specific skin conditions, it's best to consult a dermatologist before trying any DIY recipes.

As you embark on your journey towards healthier and radiant skin, remember that caring for your skin is more than just a routine; it's a gesture of self-love. With each carefully chosen product and every mindful skincare step, you're not only nurturing your skin but also nurturing your sense of confidence and well-being. So, go ahead and let your skincare routine be a testament to the beauty of self-care, as you embrace the joy of glowing, rejuvenated skin. Incorporate these principles into your skincare routine, and you'll be well on your way to achieving healthy, radiant skin. Here's to a glowing future with your revitalized skincare regimen.

Chapter 7: Conclusion

In the journey of self-development, we uncover the remarkable potential that resides within us, transcending our limitations and embracing growth with unwavering determination. This transformative pursuit is a testament to our commitment to evolve, enriching our lives with newfound wisdom, skills, and insights. As we navigate the labyrinth of self-discovery, we cultivate resilience, self-awareness, and an unyielding drive to become the best versions of ourselves. Through continuous learning, introspection, and intentional action, we forge a path that not only elevates our individuality but also contributes positively to the world around us. Self-development is not a destination but an ongoing voyage that empowers us to shape our destiny and leave an indelible mark on the canvas of existence.

7.1 Achieving Your Goals

Achieving your goals in self-development requires clear objectives, a well-defined plan, consistent effort, and adaptability. Set SMART goals for yourself—short-term, measurable, attainable, relevant, and time-bound. Break them into actionable steps and commit to regular progress. Stay motivated by visualizing success and celebrating milestones. Embrace challenges, learn from setbacks, and adjust your approach as needed. Persistence, self-discipline, and a growth mindset are key to realizing your personal development aspirations.

7.2 Stay Motivated

To stay motivated, you need to set clear goals, break them into smaller achievable tasks, and celebrate milestones. Maintain a positive mindset, focus on your progress, and embrace failures as learning opportunities. Consistent routines, seeking inspiration, and surrounding yourself with supportive people can also help sustain motivation. Know that motivation is a skill you can cultivate through discipline and perseverance.

7.3 Celebrate Your Achievements

It is an essential practice that fosters motivation, confidence, and growth. When you acknowledge and commemorate your accomplishments, you reinforce positive behaviors and cultivate a mindset of success. These celebrations provide a sense of validation, serving as tangible reminders of your progress and hard work. Such recognition not only boosts self-esteem but also encourages you to set new goals and continue pursuing personal growth. By taking time to revel in your achievements, you create a cycle of positivity that fuels continuous self-improvement. Remember, celebrating your successes is not about arrogance, but about acknowledging your journey and the strides you've made towards becoming the best version of yourself.

7.4 Stay on Track With Your Goals

Staying on track with your goals is a cornerstone of personal and professional success. The ability to set, pursue, and ultimately achieve one's objectives requires a combination of discipline, focus, and effective strategies. To ensure goal attainment, individuals can implement several key practices that contribute to sustained progress.

First and foremost, setting clear and well-defined goals is imperative. The SMART framework provides a roadmap for measuring progress and maintaining motivation. Additionally, articulating the "why" behind each goal fosters a deeper sense of purpose, enhancing commitment and resilience when faced with challenges.

Maintaining focus is a critical component of goal pursuit. The modern world is replete with distractions, making it essential to cultivate techniques that enhance concentration. Employing strategies such as time blocking, minimizing multitasking, and creating a dedicated workspace can bolster productivity and limit diversions.

Accountability mechanisms can significantly contribute to goal adherence. Sharing goals with a mentor, coach, or an accountability partner creates a sense of responsibility and encourages consistent effort. Regular check-ins enable the assessment of progress, identification of potential obstacles, and recalibration if necessary.

Inevitably, setbacks and challenges will arise. However, reframing these obstacles as opportunities for growth can alter one's perspective. Embracing a resilient mindset, characterized by adaptability and perseverance, fosters the tenacity required to navigate through difficulties and emerge stronger.

In conclusion, staying on track with your goals demands a holistic approach encompassing clear goal-setting, strategic planning, focused execution, accountability, and resilience in the face of adversity. By adhering to these practices and maintaining a proactive mindset, individuals can enhance their likelihood of accomplishing their aspirations, both personally and professionally. Remember, the journey towards goal attainment is a continuous process that requires dedication, patience, and consistent effort.

Imagine disappearing for six months and coming back as the best version of yourself, your soul reawakened, and your spirit rejuvenated. Armed with newfound clarity and vitality, you'd approach life's ventures with unwavering optimism and an invigorated sense of direction, inspiring everyone you encounter with the transformative power of self-discovery. So, get activated, make every step count, and the skies will only be your starting point!